THE AUSTRALIAN
Women's Weekly

VEG IT UP!

CONTENTS

LESS MEAT MORE VEG

Why be a vegetarian?

People choose to follow a vegetarian diet for ethical, health or for a myriad of other reasons. If being a vegetarian is a religious or ethical choice, the decision on diet should be easy and in the case of religion, it's usually a tradition-based choice. An ethical choice can be based on many philosophies. Some simply don't want to eat any animal products at all. Others also genuinely care about where their food comes from – when and how it was grown and the journey it takes to arrive in stores. These people are concerned about the footprint that's left on the planet, long after they've left it. Choosing to eat all or even mostly plant foods will leave the lightest footprint of all on our precious planet. As we become more health conscious and socially aware about where our food comes from, going meat-free is becoming a mainstream choice.

Health benefits

There are many health benefits to following a well-balanced, properly-researched vegetarian diet. A vegetarian diet is nothing new. Vast numbers of people around the world have been following a plant-based diet for centuries, and mostly live longer than their meat-eating counterparts, carry less body fat and are at a lower risk of developing type-2 diabetes, heart disease, and some cancers. Teeth and gums get a good work-out as lots of chewing is involved. The happy feeling of having had plenty to eat can be achieved easily, providing the food is chewed properly – chewing slows most eaters down, so giving the body time to reach that 'full' feeling – about 20 minutes, we're told. Most digestive problems disappear with a healthy vegetarian diet; the digestive tract and gut actually like a bit of hard work and will respond kindly. This is because a well-balanced vegetarian diet includes a wide array of plant matter, fibre and tends to be low fat. As with any diet however, it is possible to make it unbalanced by eating too much dairy, fatty or high sugar foods.

Vegetarianism

Within the world of vegetarianism there are various sub groups:

Lacto-ovo vegetarians eat dairy products and eggs.	**Lacto- vegetarians** eat dairy but not eggs.	**Ovo- vegetarians** eat eggs but not dairy.	**Vegans** strictest of vegetarians, abstaining from all animal products, including dairy, eggs and even honey.	**Flexitarians** eat some white meat and/or fish.	**Pollo vegetarians** eat some white meat such as poultry.

Making the switch

As with anything new, allowing for a period of transition will increase your chances of making a lasting change. With this in mind, the recipes in the A Touch of Protein chapter contain a little seafood and white meat – pork and chicken. Each recipe also comes with a tip on how to 'Veg It Up!', modifying the meal to become vegetarian, as you become used to eating less meat in your everyday diet.

Purely Veg is full of substantial no-fuss meatless meals some with dairy and eggs, that you can enjoy every day of the week. Finally, Power Salads & Sides provides great vegie-packed accompaniments to add a vegetable boost to your dishes, helping you put the emphasis on plant-based foods in every meal. With our delicious recipes you won't even notice the absence of meat from your dinner.

Changing habits

It's really important to make a sensible decision if you're changing your eating habits. The diet must be balanced for good health and vitality and include a wide variety of foods which contain iron, vitamins, minerals, fibre, protein, 'good' fat, carbohydrates, natural sugars etc.

If in doubt, consult with a nutritionist, dietitian or medical practitioner – choose one who is sympathetic to vegetarianism as a way of life.

Even if you don't already follow a vegetarian diet completely, it's a good idea to increase your plant-based foods and eat less meat. The health benefits will reveal themselves to you in a very short space of time. You'll look and feel better and wonder why you didn't make the change years ago. (See inside front flap for Nutritional Needs.)

A TOUCH OF PROTEIN

For the meat-eater who would like to add more plant foods to their diet. These recipes contain lots of vegies and some white meat and fish. They also have tips on how to swap out the animal-based protein to make your meal vegetarian.

KALE CAESAR SALAD

INGREDIENTS

1 litre (4 cups) water

4 sprigs fresh thyme

2 cloves garlic, crushed

½ medium lemon (70g), sliced thinly

400g (12½ ounces) free-range chicken breast fillets

12 thin slices sourdough baguette (100g)

¾ cup (60g) finely grated parmesan

1 tablespoon olive oil

8 free-range middle bacon slices (240g)

1 teaspoon white vinegar

4 free-range eggs

240g (7½ ounces) baby kale leaves

GREEN GODDESS DRESSING

¼ cup (75g) whole-egg mayonnaise

2 tablespoons sour cream

¼ cup coarsely chopped fresh flat-leaf parsley

1 tablespoon coarsely chopped fresh basil

1 tablespoon coarsely chopped fresh chives

2 tablespoons water

1 tablespoon lemon juice

1 drained anchovy fillet, chopped coarsely

1 clove garlic, chopped finely

METHOD

1 Bring the water, thyme sprigs, garlic and lemon to the boil in a medium saucepan. Add chicken, return to the boil. Reduce heat; simmer, uncovered, for 12 minutes or until chicken is cooked through. Remove chicken; cool 10 minutes, then shred coarsely. Reserve poaching liquid for another use (see tips).

2 Meanwhile, make green goddess dressing.

3 Preheat grill (broiler). Toast bread on one side, then turn and sprinkle with half the parmesan; grill croutons until parmesan melts and is browned lightly.

4 Heat oil in a small frying pan over medium heat, cook bacon until golden and crisp; drain on paper towel.

5 Half fill a large saucepan with water; bring to the boil. Add vinegar to water. Break one 1 egg into a cup then slide into pan; repeat with remaining eggs. When eggs are in pan, return to the boil. Cover pan, turn off heat; stand 3 minutes or until a light film of egg white sets over the yolks.

6 Meanwhile, place kale and one-quarter of the dressing in a large bowl; toss to combine. Stand for 5 minutes to soften slightly.

7 Add croutons, bacon, remaining parmesan and dressing; toss to combine. Serve salad topped with poached egg. Season.

GREEN GODDESS DRESSING Blend or process all ingredients until smooth; season to taste. (Makes ¾ cup)

TIPS   The poaching liquid in step 1 can be used as a light chicken stock for another recipe. Allow to cool; refrigerate and use within 2 days, or freeze for up to 1 month. Dressing can be made up to 3 days ahead; keep tightly covered in the fridge.

SERVES 4

PREP + COOK TIME 45 MINUTES (+ COOLING)

VEG IT UP!

Leave out the chicken and bacon, and add a coarsely chopped avocado. Omit the anchovy.

Dark leafy greens such as kale provide a rich supply of A and C vitamins, fibre and phytonutrients that may be useful to prevent heart disease and cancer.

VEG
IT UP!
Swap chicken schnitzels
for thickly sliced
eggplant or
haloumi.

CHICKEN SCHNITZEL BUNS WITH APPLE SLAW

INGREDIENTS

300g (9½ ounces) stale sourdough bread, torn coarsely

6 thin free-range chicken schnitzels (850g)

½ cup (75g) plain (all-purpose) flour

2 free-range eggs, beaten lightly

2 tablespoons olive oil

60g (2 ounces) butter, chopped coarsely

6 brioche buns (540g)

¼ cup (75g) aïoli

APPLE SLAW

¼ cup (60ml) buttermilk

1 tablespoon olive oil

2 teaspoons dijon mustard

1 tablespoon lemon juice

1 teaspoon caraway seeds, toasted, crushed coarsely

2 cups (160g) shredded purple cabbage

½ medium red apple (75g), cut into matchsticks

½ baby fennel bulb (65g), sliced thinly, fronds reserved

1 cup loosely packed fresh flat-leaf parsley leaves, torn

METHOD

1 Make apple slaw.

2 Process sourdough until fine crumbs form. Transfer to an oven tray. Coat chicken in flour; shake away excess. Dip chicken in egg, then coat in breadcrumbs.

3 Preheat oven to 120°C/250°F. Line an oven tray with baking paper.

4 Heat half the oil and half the butter in a large frying pan over medium-high; cook chicken for 2 minutes each side or until golden and cooked through. Transfer to tray; keep warm in oven. Repeat with remaining oil, butter and schnitzels. Halve schnitzels.

5 Split buns in half. Spread bun bases with aïoli; top with halved schnitzel, apple slaw and bun tops.

APPLE SLAW Combine buttermilk, oil, mustard and juice in a large bowl; season to taste. Add seeds, cabbage, apple, fennel, reserved fronds and parsley; toss to combine.

TIPS We used pink lady apples in this recipe, or you could use a green variety. You could also use panko (Japanese) breadcrumbs instead of making your own.

MAKES 6

PREP + COOK TIME 45 MINUTES

BROCCOLINI, ASPARAGUS & MISO CHICKEN SALAD

Miso is a living fermented product that's good for gut health. It also contains naturally occurring glutamates, making it deliciously moreish.

INGREDIENTS

2 tablespoons white miso (shiro) paste

2 tablespoons mirin

2 tablespoons olive oil

400g (12½ ounces) free-range chicken breast fillets, halved horizontally

200g (6½ ounces) broccolini, halved lengthways

170g (5½ ounces) asparagus, trimmed, halved on the diagonal

½ cup (75g) roasted cashews, chopped coarsely

1 cup loosely packed fresh coriander (cilantro) leaves

1 cup loosely packed fresh mint leaves

CREAMY MISO DRESSING

3 teaspoons brazil and cashew nut spread

1 tablespoon white miso (shiro) paste

1 tablespoon mirin

2 teaspoons water

1 tablespoon olive oil

¼ teaspoon sesame oil

METHOD

1 Make creamy miso dressing.

2 Combine miso, mirin and half the oil in a medium bowl. Add chicken; turn to coat. Cover; refrigerate for 1 hour.

3 Boil, steam or microwave broccolini and asparagus until tender; drain. Cover to keep warm.

4 Heat remaining oil in a medium non-stick frying pan over high heat; cook chicken for 2 minutes on each side or until browned and cooked through. Cool for 5 minutes, then shred coarsely.

5 Place chicken, broccolini and asparagus in a large bowl with cashews, herbs and dressing; toss to combine.

CREAMY MISO DRESSING Place ingredients in a small screw-top jar; shake well until combined.

TIPS White miso (shiro) is sweeter and milder in taste than brown, red and black miso, making it perfect for dressings. It is available from most major supermarkets and Asian food stores. You will need 1 bunch of broccolini and 1 bunch of asparagus for this recipe.

SERVES 4

PREP + COOK TIME 25 MINUTES (+ REFRIGERATION)

VEG IT UP!

Instead of chicken, use oyster mushrooms; cook them in the pan for 3 minutes or until tender.

VEG
IT UP!

Forget the ham and
replace it with 4 slices
(170g) drained, sliced,
roasted red
capsicum.

CARAMELISED ONION, HAM & PECORINO STRATA

If you have any leftover stale bread save it to use in this savoury bread pudding. This would also be delicious served cold.

INGREDIENTS

2 tablespoons olive oil

2 medium brown onions (300g), sliced thinly

3 teaspoons finely chopped fresh rosemary

8 eggs

2 cups (500ml) milk

⅔ cup (50g) finely grated pecorino cheese or parmesan

200g (6½ ounces) shaved free-range ham, chopped coarsely

2 tablespoons smoked almonds, chopped coarsely

500g (1 pound) wholemeal sourdough bread, torn

500g (1 pound) cherry truss tomatoes

¼ cup loosely packed small fresh basil leaves

METHOD

1 Preheat oven to 200°C/400°F.

2 Heat half the oil in a large frying pan over medium-high heat; cook onion, stirring, for 15 minutes or until onion caramelises. Add rosemary; cook, stirring, for 1 minute or until fragrant.

3 Whisk eggs, milk and half the cheese in a large jug. Combine the onion mixture, ham and almonds in a medium bowl. Layer bread and ham mixture between four 2 cup (500ml) ovenproof dishes. Pour over egg mixture; sprinkle with remaining cheese. Stand for 20 minutes.

4 Bake for 35 minutes or until just set, golden and puffed.

5 Meanwhile, cut tomatoes into four clusters; place on an oven tray, drizzle with remaining oil. Roast for the last 10 minutes of strata cooking time or until skins start to split.

6 Serve strata topped with tomatoes and basil.

SERVING SUGGESTION Serve with a mixed garden salad.

SERVES 4

PREP + COOK TIME 1 HOUR (+ STANDING)

CHICKEN & POTATO STIR-FRY

This unusual Sichuan Chinese recipe features potato, an ingredient not often seen in Chinese cooking, cut into fine noodle-like strips.

INGREDIENTS

2 medium desiree potatoes (400g), cut into fine matchsticks (see tips)

½ teaspoon sea salt flakes

1 tablespoon ground cumin

2 tablespoons rice flour

2 teaspoons dried chilli flakes

300g (9½ ounces) free-range chicken breast strips

1 tablespoon sesame oil

3 cloves garlic, chopped finely

400g (12½ ounces) chinese water spinach, trimmed, cut into 10cm (4-inch) lengths

2 tablespoons light soy sauce

¼ cup (60ml) malt vinegar

½ teaspoon caster (superfine) sugar

2 fresh long green chillies, sliced thinly on the diagonal

¼ teaspoon dried chilli flakes, extra

METHOD

1 Place potatoes and salt in a large bowl, cover with cold water; stand for 15 minutes. Drain; pat dry with paper towel.

2 Meanwhile, combine cumin, flour and half the chilli flakes in a shallow bowl. Coat chicken in spice mixture; shake away excess.

3 Heat half the oil in a wok over high heat; stir-fry coated chicken for 3 minutes or until just cooked through. Remove from wok.

4 Heat remaining oil in wok over medium-high heat; stir-fry garlic and potatoes for 5 minutes or until potatoes are tender. Add spinach; cook for 1 minute or until wilted.

5 Meanwhile, combine soy sauce, vinegar, sugar and remaining chilli flakes in a small bowl; stir until sugar dissolves. Return chicken to wok with soy mixture and green chillies; stir-fry until heated through.

6 Serve stir-fry topped with coarsely chopped peanuts and coriander sprigs, if you like.

TIPS You can use any variety of waxy potatoes such as bintje and dutch cream. For less heat remove the seeds and the membrane from the chillies first.

SERVES 4

VEG
IT UP!

Replace the chicken
with tofu. Replace light
soy with tamari to also
make the stir-fry
gluten-free.

VEG IT UP!

Skip the bacon and use firm fetta chunks or corn kernels instead.

SMOKY TOMATO & BACON FRITTERS

Avocados offer a rich supply of 14 different minerals and vitamins, as well as heart-friendly monosaturated fatty acids.

INGREDIENTS

250g (8 ounces) thick bacon slices, chopped coarsely

2 cloves garlic, crushed

400g (12½ ounces) ripe tomatoes, chopped finely

2 teaspoons smoked paprika

2 tablespoons chopped fresh chives

2 free-range eggs

⅓ cup (80ml) milk

1 cup (150g) spelt flour

½ teaspoon baking powder

1 medium avocado (250g)

½ cup (150g) whole-egg mayonnaise

1 tablespoon lemon juice

1 clove garlic, crushed, extra

2 tablespoons olive oil

1 large fennel bulb (550g), sliced thinly

1 tablespoon chopped fresh chives, extra

METHOD

1 Heat a large, non-stick frying pan over high heat; cook bacon, stirring, until golden and crisp. Transfer to a large bowl.

2 Add garlic, tomato, paprika, chives, eggs and milk; stir to combine. Add combined sifted flour and baking powder; season and stir to combine. Stand mixture for 15 minutes.

3 Meanwhile, blend or process avocado flesh, mayonnaise, juice and extra garlic until smooth. Season to taste.

4 Heat oil in same frying pan over medium heat. Spoon 2 tablespoonfuls of batter into pan; cook for 2 minutes or until bubbles appear. Turn fritters; cook until other side is lightly browned. Repeat with remaining mixture to make 8 fritters in total.

5 Combine fennel and extra chives in a small bowl; season.

6 Serve fritters with fennel salad and avocado mixture.

SERVES 4

PREP + COOK TIME 40 MINUTES (+ STANDING)

BEETROOT, BLOOD ORANGE & PORK SALAD

Beets are also an excellent source of folate and a very good source of manganese, potassium and copper. Their leaves are also very nutritious.

INGREDIENTS

200g (6½ ounces) free-range pork fillet, trimmed

1 wholemeal baguette (240g), halved horizontally, halved crossways

2 tablespoons olive oil

440g (14 ounces) canned baby beetroots (beets), halved

3 small blood oranges (570g), peeled, sliced thinly

100g (3 ounces) radicchio leaves, torn

75g (2½ ounces) mixed salad leaves

8 fresh pitted dates (160g), halved

½ cup (60g) pitted kalamata olives, halved

2 tablespoons pepitas (pumpkin seed kernels), roasted

2 tablespoons sunflower seeds, roasted

2 teaspoons poppy seeds

RASPBERRY ORANGE BLOSSOM DRESSING

2 tablespoons raspberry wine vinegar

2 tablespoons olive oil

1 tablespoon orange blossom water

1 small clove garlic, crushed

2 teaspoons chopped fresh chives

METHOD

1 Make raspberry orange blossom dressing.

2 Drizzle pork and bread with oil; season. Cook pork on a lightly oiled heated grill plate (or grill or barbecue), turning frequently, for 15 minutes or until cooked through. Rest, loosely covered, for 5 minutes before slicing thickly. Place bread on the oiled heated grill plate for 2 minutes each side or until golden. Tear bread into large pieces.

3 Place pork in a large bowl with beetroot, blood oranges, radicchio, salad leaves, dates, olives and dressing; toss to combine. Sprinkle salad with seeds, serve with bread.

RASPBERRY ORANGE BLOSSOM DRESSING Combine ingredients in a small bowl; season to taste.

TIPS Dressing, without chives, can be made up to 2 days ahead; keep refrigerated. Add chives just before serving.

When blood oranges are out of season use regular oranges.

Use grilled chicken breast or thigh fillets instead of the pork, if you like.

SERVES 4

PREP + COOK TIME 40 MINUTES

VEG IT UP!

Give the pork a miss and use grilled haloumi slices instead.

VEG
IT UP!

Replace the chicken
with pan-fried
haloumi slices.

LEMON THYME CHICKEN WITH CAPERBERRY SALSA

Chicken breast supreme is a chicken breast with the skin and wing bone attached. You can use skinless chicken breast fillets instead.

INGREDIENTS

4 free-range chicken breast supreme (1kg) (see note above)

¼ cup (60ml) olive oil

2 tablespoons fresh thyme leaves

1 tablespoon finely grated lemon rind

1 celeriac (celery root) (750g), peeled

2 large carrots (360g)

1 clove garlic, crushed

2 tablespoons white balsamic vinegar

½ cup (100g) roasted pepitas (pumpkin seed kernels)

¾ cup coarsely chopped fresh flat-leaf parsley

2 tablespoons greek-style yoghurt

¼ cup fresh flat-leaf parsley leaves, extra

¼ cup fresh thyme sprigs, extra

CAPERBERRY SALSA

1 cup (160g) caperberries

2 tablespoons olive oil

2 tablespoons lemon juice

1½ teaspoons dried pink peppercorns, crushed coarsely

SERVES 4

PREP + COOK TIME 50 MINUTES (+ STANDING)

METHOD

1 Preheat oven to 220°C/425°F. Line an oven tray with baking paper.

2 Combine chicken, 1 tablespoon oil, thyme and rind in a large bowl; stand for 10 minutes.

3 Meanwhile, using a vegetable peeler, peel long thin ribbons from the celeriac and carrot (keep the centre core of each vegetable for another use, see tip). Place vegetable ribbons in a large bowl with garlic, vinegar, pepitas, chopped parsley and yoghurt; season. Stir to combine.

4 Heat a large frying pan over medium-high heat; cook chicken for 3 minutes each side or until browned all over. Transfer to tray; roast for 12 minutes or until cooked through.

5 Meanwhile, make caperberry salsa.

6 Serve chicken with vegetable salad and salsa; top with extra parsley and thyme.

CAPERBERRY SALSA Halve three-quarters of the caperberries, keeping the stems attached; reserve remaining for serving. Combine halved caperberries in a small bowl with oil, juice and peppercorns.

TIP You can use the remaining centre core of the celeriac and carrot in a soup.

ROAST TROUT, FENNEL & BUCKWHEAT SALAD

INGREDIENTS

3 baby fennel (390g), trimmed, fronds reserved

¼ cup (60ml) lemon juice

¼ cup (60ml) olive oil

1 small clove garlic, chopped finely

1 tablespoon finely grated lemon rind (see tip)

3 skinless ocean trout fillets (660g)

1 cup (200g) buckwheat

1 cup loosely packed fresh flat-leaf parsley leaves, torn

CORIANDER LEMON DRESSING

2 teaspoons coriander seeds

½ cup loosely packed fresh coriander (cilantro) leaves

⅓ cup (80ml) lemon juice

2 tablespoons extra virgin olive oil

1 small clove garlic, chopped finely

½ teaspoon smoked paprika

METHOD

1 Preheat oven to 180°C/350°F. Line two oven trays with baking paper.

2 Cut two fennel bulbs into thin wedges; place on a tray. Thinly slice remaining fennel. Combine sliced fennel and 1 tablespoon of the juice in a small bowl.

3 Whisk oil, garlic, rind and remaining juice in a small jug; season to taste. Drizzle half the lemon mixture over fennel wedges; roast for 35 minutes or until tender.

4 Meanwhile, place trout on second tray; drizzle with remaining lemon mixture. Roast for 12 minutes or until almost cooked through; flake coarsely.

5 Heat a medium frying pan over medium heat; toast buckwheat, stirring, until light golden.

6 Cook buckwheat in a medium saucepan of boiling water for 20 minutes or until tender; drain. Cool slightly.

7 Meanwhile, make coriander lemon dressing.

8 Place roasted fennel, sliced fennel, reserved fennel fronds, trout, buckwheat, parsley and dressing in a large bowl; toss to combine. Season to taste.

CORIANDER LEMON DRESSING Place coriander seeds in a small frying pan, stir over medium heat for 2 minutes or until fragrant and toasted; cool. Grind seeds coarsely with a pestle and mortar. Process ground coriander seeds with remaining ingredients until smooth and combined. Season to taste.

TIP For this recipe, you will need to grate the rind from 2 or 3 lemons before juicing.

SERVES 4

PREP + COOK TIME 1 HOUR 15 MINUTES

VEG
IT UP!

Replace the fish with
pan-fried haloumi
slices.

BEER-BATTERED FISH WITH JALAPEÑO & WATERMELON SALAD

We used snapper in this recipe but you could use any firm white fish you prefer, such as ling or whiting.

INGREDIENTS

1¼ cups (185g) self-raising flour

⅔ cup (160ml) chilled beer

2 teaspoons garlic salt

vegetable oil, for deep-frying

400g (12½ ounces) firm white fish fillets, cut into thick strips (see note above)

2 pitta breads

JALAPEÑO & WATERMELON SALAD

2 fresh jalapeño chillies, sliced thinly

1 small red onion (100g), sliced thinly

1 clove garlic, sliced thinly

2 tablespoons white wine vinegar

1 tablespoon caster (superfine) sugar

500g (1 pound) seedless watermelon, chopped coarsely

1 baby cos (romaine) lettuce (200g), trimmed, leaves separated

2 small avocados (400g), sliced thinly

1 cup loosely packed fresh coriander (cilantro) leaves

2 tablespoons lime juice

1 tablespoon olive oil

METHOD

1 Whisk ¾ cup of the flour, the beer and garlic salt in a medium bowl to form a thick batter; refrigerate 15 minutes.

2 Meanwhile, make jalapeño and watermelon salad.

3 Fill a wok one-third with oil and heat to 180°C/350°F (or until a cube of bread browns in 15 seconds). Place remaining flour in a medium bowl. Coat fish in flour; shake away excess. Dip fish in batter; drain off excess. Deep-fry fish, in batches, until golden and cooked through. Drain on paper towel.

4 Serve fish immediately with salad and pitta bread.

JALAPEÑO & WATERMELON SALAD Combine jalapeños, onion, garlic, vinegar and sugar in a large bowl; stand 10 minutes. Strain jalapeño mixture; discard liquid. Return jalapeño mixture to bowl. Add watermelon, lettuce, avocado, coriander, juice and oil; toss to combine.

SERVES 4

PREP + COOK TIME 50 MINUTES

TUNA SALAD SUSHI BOWL

This salad bowl has all the ingredients of a sushi roll, but with the added health benefits of unhulled brown rice.

INGREDIENTS

⅓ cup (80ml) teriyaki sauce

⅓ cup (80ml) rice vinegar

1 tablespoon finely grated fresh ginger

450g (14½ ounces) packaged brown microwave rice

2 x 185g (6 ounces) cans tuna in springwater, drained

1 lebanese cucumber (130g), halved lengthways, seeded, sliced thinly lengthways

1 large avocado (320g), sliced thinly

1 large carrot (180g), cut into matchsticks

⅓ cup (90g) drained pickled ginger, sliced thinly

1 tablespoon sesame seeds, toasted

½ sheet toasted seaweed (nori), shredded finely

METHOD

1 To make dressing, combine sauce, vinegar and ginger in a small bowl.

2 Reheat rice following packet instructions.

3 Combine warm rice and half the dressing in a bowl.

4 Serve rice with tuna, cucumber, avocado, carrot and pickled ginger. Drizzle with remaining dressing; sprinkle with sesame seeds and seaweed.

SERVES 4

PREP + COOK TIME 35 MINUTES

FISH BÁNH MÌ WITH PICKLED VEGETABLES & SPICY MAYONNAISE

Bánh mì is actually a Vietnamese term for all kinds of bread, but has become synonymous with a Vietnamese-style sandwich.

INGREDIENTS

2 teaspoons peanut oil

2 teaspoons sesame oil

8 small flathead fillets (880g)

2 half baguettes (300g), ends trimmed, halved crossways

1 lebanese cucumber (130g), halved lengthways, seeded, sliced thinly

1 green onion (scallion), sliced thinly on the diagonal

1 fresh long red chilli, sliced thinly

8 large fresh coriander (cilantro) sprigs

PICKLED VEGETABLES

½ cup (110g) white (granulated) sugar

½ cup (125ml) rice vinegar

½ teaspoon coarse cooking (kosher) salt

1 medium carrot (120g), cut into matchsticks

¼ medium daikon (150g), cut into matchsticks

SPICY MAYONNAISE

¼ cup (75g) whole-egg mayonnaise

3 teaspoons sriracha or other chilli sauce

METHOD

1 Make pickled vegetables and spicy mayonnaise.

2 Heat oils in a large frying pan over high heat; cook fish fillets for 2½ minutes each side or until just cooked through.

3 Split baguettes in half horizontally. Spread mayonnaise over bases; top with fish, cucumber, green onion, pickled vegetables, chilli and coriander.

PICKLED VEGETABLES Stir sugar, vinegar and salt in a small saucepan over low heat for 2 minutes or until sugar dissolves; bring to the boil. Transfer mixture to a medium bowl; stir in carrot and daikon. Refrigerate for 1 hour. Drain.

SPICY MAYONNAISE Combine ingredients in a small bowl; season to taste. Refrigerate until required.

TIP Sriracha is a medium-hot chilli sauce available from Asian food stores and some major supermarkets.

SERVES 4

PREP + COOK TIME 35 MINUTES (+ REFRIGERATION)

MUSSELS IN CHILLI BROTH WITH FREEKEH

Freekeh is made from roasted young green wheat – it has a low GI, four times the fibre of brown rice and is high in protein.

INGREDIENTS

1 cup (250ml) dry white wine

1kg (2 pounds) black mussels, cleaned (see tips)

1 tablespoon olive oil

1 medium brown onion (150g), chopped finely

2 stalks celery (300g), trimmed, cut into 1cm (½-inch) pieces

400g (12½ ounces) baby (dutch) carrots, sliced thinly on the diagonal

2 tablespoons tomato paste

1 cup (170g) wheat freekeh, rinsed (see tips)

½ teaspoon dried chilli flakes

3 cups (750ml) fish stock

1 medium lemon (140g), cut into wedges

2 tablespoons coarsely chopped fresh flat-leaf parsley

METHOD

1 Bring wine to the boil in a large saucepan over medium-high heat. Add mussels; cook, covered, for 8 minutes or until mussels open. Strain mussels through a colander into a large heatproof bowl; reserve cooking liquid. Cover mussels; refrigerate until required.

2 Heat oil in same saucepan over medium heat; cook onion, celery and carrots for 3 minutes or until onion softens. Add paste, freekeh and chilli; cook, stirring, for 1 minute or until fragrant. Add stock and reserved cooking liquid; bring to the boil. Reduce heat; simmer, partially covered, for 1 hour until freekeh is tender.

3 Add mussels to pan; cook, uncovered, for 2 minutes or until heated through. Serve mussels with lemon wedges and topped with parsley.

TIPS If you prefer, you can buy a 1kg (2-pound) pack of pot-ready mussels from fishmongers or seafood markets. These are already scrubbed and bearded, and ready to cook. Some mussels might not open after cooking. These might need prompting with a knife or might not have cooked as quickly as the others - some will not open after excessive cooking. You do not have to discard these, just open with a knife and cook a little more if you like

You can use vongole (clams) instead of the mussels.

Freekeh is available at health food shops, some delicatessens and greengrocers. Freekeh does contain gluten so is not suitable for those on gluten-free diets.

SERVES 4

PREP + COOK TIME 1 HOUR 35 MINUTES

VEG
IT UP!

Replace prawns with
asparagus and assorted
asian mushrooms; use
a mushroom-based
vegetarian oyster
sauce.

BLACK PEPPER, TOFU & PRAWNS

This dish uses the flavours traditionally used to make Singaporean chilli crab. Serve with steamed jasmine rice or warmed roti.

INGREDIENTS

300g (9½ ounces) firm tofu, cut into 3cm (1¼-inch) pieces

2 tablespoons coconut oil

12 uncooked medium king prawns (shrimp) (500g), peeled, deveined, tails intact

175g (5½ ounces) green beans, cut into 5cm (2-inch) lengths

2 tablespoons drained fermented black beans, rinsed, chopped coarsely

1½ teaspoons black peppercorns, ground coarsely (see tip)

2 cloves garlic, sliced thinly

20g (¾-ounce) piece fresh ginger, cut into matchsticks

2 tablespoons oyster sauce

1 teaspoon caster (superfine) sugar

2 tablespoons water

3 green onions (scallions), sliced thinly

1 fresh small red chilli, sliced thinly

METHOD

1 Place tofu in between paper towel; stand for 30 minutes.

2 Heat oil in a wok over high heat; stir-fry prawns and beans for 2 minutes or until prawns are almost cooked through. Add black beans, pepper, garlic, ginger, sauce, sugar and the water; stir-fry for 1 minute or until combined. Add tofu and green onion; stir-fry for 1 minute or until heated through.

3 Serve immediately topped with chilli.

TIP To grind pepper coarsely, loosen the tension on your pepper mill to produce a coarser grind or alternatively use a mortar and pestle.

SERVES 4

PREP + COOK TIME 35 MINUTES (+ STANDING)

SPANISH-STYLE FISH WITH SMOKY EGGPLANT

We used whiting fillets in this recipe but you could use any firm white fish fillets, such as snapper or bream.

INGREDIENTS

4 small eggplants (400g)

1 medium red capsicum (bell pepper) (200g)

1 teaspoon smoked paprika

2 tablespoons olive oil

8 whiting fillets (960g) (see note above)

400g (12½ ounces) canned cannellini beans, drained, rinsed

½ cup (150g) whole-egg mayonnaise

1 clove garlic, crushed

1 tablespoon lemon juice

1 medium lemon (140g), cut into wedges

2 tablespoons coarsely chopped fresh flat-leaf parsley

METHOD

1 Preheat oven to 200°C/400°F. Line an oven tray with baking paper.

2 Cut eggplant in half lengthways; score the flesh. Quarter capsicum; discard seeds and membranes. Place eggplant and capsicum, skin-side up, on the tray. Roast for 30 minutes or until capsicum skin blisters and blackens and eggplant is tender. Transfer to a heatproof bowl; cover with plastic wrap for 5 minutes, then peel away vegetable skins. Shred eggplant coarsely; chop capsicum coarsely. Season to taste.

3 Meanwhile, combine smoked paprika and half the oil in a medium shallow bowl; add fish, turn to coat. Heat a large non-stick frying pan over high heat; cook fish, in two batches, skin-side first, for 1½ minutes each side or until just cooked through. Transfer to a plate; cover to keep warm.

4 Heat remaining oil in same pan over medium heat; cook beans, stirring, until warmed through. Season to taste.

5 Meanwhile, combine mayonnaise, garlic and juice in a small bowl; season to taste.

6 Serve fish with eggplant, capsicum, beans, aïoli and lemon wedges; top with parsley.

SERVES 4

PREP + COOK TIME 55 MINUTES

VEG
IT UP!

Use eggplant or orange
sweet potato instead
of the fish.

FISH SKEWERS WITH LABNE & CHILLI TOMATO SALAD

Preserved lemon is available at delicatessens and some supermarkets. Remove and discard the flesh, rinse rind, then use as recipe directs.

INGREDIENTS

400g (12½ ounces) firm white fish fillets, cut into 2.5cm (1-inch) pieces (see tips)

1 tablespoon garlic oil

½ teaspoon ground sumac

280g (9 ounces) labne

2 tablespoons roasted flaked almonds

CHILLI TOMATO SALAD

400g (12½ ounces) mixed baby heirloom tomatoes, chopped coarsely

1 tablespoon thinly sliced preserved lemon rind (see notes above)

1 fresh long red chilli, seeded, sliced thinly

1 cup loosely packed fresh flat-leaf parsley leaves

½ cup loosely packed fresh mint leaves

2 tablespoons red wine vinegar

1 tablespoon garlic oil

METHOD

1 Place fish and oil in a medium bowl; toss to coat. Thread fish onto four skewers; season.

2 Heat a large non-stick frying pan over high heat; cook fish for 3 minutes each side or until just cooked through. Sprinkle with sumac.

3 Meanwhile, make chilli tomato salad.

4 Serve fish on salad with labne; top with almonds.

CHILLI TOMATO SALAD Combine all ingredients in a large bowl. Season to taste.

TIPS We used blue eye trevalla in this recipe but you can use any firm white fish you prefer. You could use 2 teaspoons finely grated lemon rind instead of preserved lemon rind.

SERVES 4

PREP + COOK TIME 30 MINUTES

FOUR WAYS WITH EGGS

EGGS WITH ASPARAGUS

Place 2 room temperature eggs in a small saucepan with enough cold water to cover; bring to the boil over medium heat. Boil for 3 minutes for a soft-boiled egg (start timing from boiling point). Drain. Meanwhile, brush 375g (12oz) asparagus, halved crossways, with a little oil; char-grill, turning occasionally, for 6 minutes or until tender. Sprinkle with 2 tablespoons dukkah. Serve soft-boiled eggs in egg cups with asparagus soldiers.

SERVES 2

PREP + COOK TIME 12 MINUTES

LAZY KALE TORTILLA

Preheat oven to 200°C/400°F. Pulse 3 cups kale leaves in a food processor until coarsely chopped; transfer to a large bowl. Repeat with 1 cup each flat-leaf parsley leaves and dill sprigs and 3 green onions; transfer to bowl. Add 9 eggs and 2 slices torn wholemeal bread; mix to combine. Season. Heat a 26cm (10½in) ovenproof frying pan over medium heat. When pan is hot, add 2 tablespoons olive oil then egg mixture; cook for 8 minutes or until tortilla is three-quarters set. Transfer to oven; cook a further 15 minutes or until set. Serve tortilla drizzled with olive oil, extra parsley and lemon wedges.

SERVES 4

PREP + COOK TIME 30 MINUTES

ASPARAGUS OMELETTE

Peel 375g (12oz) asparagus into thin ribbons; combine with
1 tablespoon each finely shredded preserved lemon rind, capers,
lemon juice, extra virgin olive oil and 2 tablespoons dill. Season.
Crumble 100g (3oz) goat's cheese. Whisk 4 eggs and 2 tablespoons
water in a jug until frothy; season. Heat 2 teaspoons olive oil in a
20cm (8in) frying pan, add half the egg; cook over medium heat
until omelette just begins to set around the edge. Top with half the
asparagus salad and half the cheese. Remove from pan. Repeat with
2 teaspoons oil, remaining egg mixture, asparagus salad and cheese.

SERVES 2

PREP + COOK TIME 15 MINUTES

EGG & SPROUT SALAD

Place 4 room temperature eggs in a small saucepan with enough cold
water to cover; bring to the boil over medium heat. Boil for 4 minutes
for slightly gooey eggs (start timing from boiling point). Drain; cool
under cold water. Peel eggs. Place leaves from 2 witlof (belgian endive)
and ½ radicchio on a platter with 1 thinly sliced celery heart (including
the leaves), 1 cup crunchy sprouts combo and 1 large (180g) shaved
carrot. Top salad with torn eggs. Combine 2 tablespoons each olive
oil and lemon juice, 1 teaspoon honey and 1 crushed clove garlic in
a screw-top jar; shake well. Season to taste. Drizzle over salad.

SERVES 2

PREP + COOK TIME 15 MINUTES

PURELY VEG

For the vegetarian who is happy to eat eggs and dairy foods. These recipes contain no meat or seafood, but instead are packed to the brim with delectable fruits, vegetables, legumes, nuts and seeds, guaranteed to satisfy. Using fresh herbs and a multitude of spices and flavours, you won't even notice the meat missing from your plate.

SPICED CARROT & SWEET POTATO SOUP

Cooling the soup for 10 minutes before blending
is essential. The heat build-up can cause the lid to blow off.

INGREDIENTS

2 tablespoons olive oil

2 medium brown onions (300g),
chopped coarsely

5 medium carrots (600g),
chopped coarsely

3 small orange sweet potatoes (750g),
chopped coarsely

1 tablespoon ground coriander

2 teaspoons cumin seeds

½ teaspoon dried chilli flakes

1 litre (4 cups) vegetable stock

2 cups (500ml) water

¾ cup (200g) greek-style yoghurt

½ cup firmly packed fresh coriander
(cilantro) sprigs

METHOD

1 Heat oil in a large saucepan over medium-high heat; cook onion, carrot and sweet potato, stirring, for 5 minutes or until onion softens. Add ground coriander, cumin and chilli; cook, stirring, for 1 minute or until fragrant.

2 Add stock and the water to pan; bring to the boil. Reduce heat; simmer, covered, for 30 minutes or until vegetables are tender. Cool soup for 10 minutes.

3 Blend soup, in batches, until smooth. Return to pan; stir over medium-high heat until heated through. Season to taste.

4 Ladle soup into bowls; top with yoghurt and coriander. Sprinkle with freshly ground black pepper.

SERVING SUGGESTION Serve with warm naan bread.

SERVES 4

PREP + COOK TIME 50 MINUTES

VEGAN

Use a vegan puff pastry and omit the egg. Use a soy or vegan yoghurt.

SPICED LENTIL & SWEET POTATO PIES

INGREDIENTS

2 tablespoons olive oil

1 medium red onion (170g),
   chopped finely

3 cloves garlic, chopped finely

1 celery stalk (150g), trimmed,
   chopped finely

2 tablespoons harissa (see tips)

1 teaspoon ground cumin

1 teaspoon ground coriander

2¼ cups (450g) french-style
   green lentils

2 small orange sweet potatoes (500g),
   cut into 3cm (1¼-inch) pieces

2 cups (500ml) vegetable stock

½ cup (125ml) water

400g (12½ ounces) canned cherry
   tomatoes in juice

60g (2 ounces) baby spinach leaves

½ cup fresh flat-leaf parsley leaves

½ cup fresh coriander (cilantro) leaves

1½ teaspoons finely grated lemon rind

4 sheets puff pastry

1 free-range egg, beaten lightly

HERB & LEMON YOGHURT

1 cup (280g) greek-style yoghurt

¼ cup coarsely chopped fresh
   flat-leaf parsley

¼ cup coarsely chopped fresh
   coriander (cilantro)

1 tablespoon finely chopped preserved
   lemon rind

1 tablespoon lemon juice

METHOD

1 Heat oil in a large saucepan over medium heat; cook onion, garlic and celery for 5 minutes or until onion softens. Add harissa, cumin and ground coriander; cook, stirring, for 1 minute or until fragrant. Add lentils, sweet potato, stock and the water; bring to the boil. Reduce heat, simmer, covered, for 20 minutes or until lentils and sweet potato are tender.

2 Add tomatoes; return to a simmer, cook, uncovered, for 5 minutes or until thickened. Stir in spinach, parsley, fresh coriander and rind; season to taste; cool.

3 Meanwhile, make herb and lemon yoghurt.

4 Preheat oven to 200°C/400°F. Grease eight 1 cup (250ml) pie tins (with a base measurement of 7.5cm/3 inches and a top measurement of 12.5cm/5 inches).

5 Cut each pastry sheet into four squares. Cut each square in half diagonally to form 32 triangles. Refrigerate until required.

6 Fill pie tins with cooled lentil filling; top each tin with four overlapping pastry triangles, pressing edges to seal. Brush tops with egg.

7 Bake pies for 30 minutes or until pastry is golden and filling is hot. Serve with herb and lemon yoghurt.

HERB & LEMON YOGHURT Combine all ingredients in a bowl.

TIPS Harissa is a hot chilli paste; there are many different brands available on the market, and the strengths vary enormously. If you have a low heat-level tolerance, you may find this, and any other recipe containing harissa, too hot to tolerate, even if you reduce the amount. Preserved lemon is available at delicatessens and some supermarkets. Remove and discard the flesh, rinse the rind, then use it as the recipe directs.

SERVES 8

PREP + COOK TIME 1 HOUR 20 MINUTES (+ COOLING)

RICE CAKES WITH ZUCCHINI & MUSHROOMS

Seaweed is a powerhouse of nutrition, rich in protein, magnesium, calcium, iron and antioxidants such as vitamin C.

INGREDIENTS

3 cups (600g) brown rice, rinsed, drained

1.25 litres (5 cups) water

1 tablespoon mirin

2 tablespoons light soy sauce

1 teaspoon caster (superfine) sugar

¼ cup (60ml) rice vinegar

2½ tablespoons sesame oil

2 green onions (scallions), sliced thinly

150g (4½ ounces) shiitake mushrooms, sliced thickly

150g (4½ ounces) shimeji mushrooms, separated

2 medium zucchini (240g), cut into matchsticks

150g (5½ ounces) snow peas, trimmed

1 sheet toasted seaweed (nori), sliced thinly

METHOD

1 Bring rice and the water to the boil in a large saucepan over medium-high heat. Reduce heat; simmer, covered, for 30 minutes or until rice is just tender. Remove from heat; stand, covered, until cool enough to handle.

2 Meanwhile, combine mirin, sauce, sugar, vinegar and 2 teaspoons of the oil in a small bowl.

3 Place half the rice, half the white part of the green onion and 1 teaspoon of the oil in a food processor; pulse until rice is coarsely chopped and sticky. Transfer rice mixture to a large bowl. Repeat with remaining rice, white part of the green onion and another 1 teaspoon of oil. Stir rice mixture to combine. Shape rice mixture into 16 patties. Brush rice cakes with 1 tablespoon of the oil.

4 Heat a large frying pan over medium heat; cook rice cakes, in batches, for 5 minutes each side or until golden and crisp.

5 Meanwhile, heat remaining oil in a wok or large frying pan over medium-high heat; cook mushrooms, stirring occasionally, until almost tender. Add zucchini and peas; cook, stirring, for 1 minute or until tender. Stir in mirin mixture.

6 Serve rice cakes with stir-fried vegetables, sprinkled with seaweed and remaining green onion.

SERVES 4

PREP + COOK TIME 1 HOUR

BROCCOLI, MUSTARD & CHEDDAR HAND PIES

Serve these hand pies with a simple green salad. They would also make a great filler for a school or work lunchbox.

INGREDIENTS

6 sheets puff pastry

½ cup (140g) honey mustard

300g (9½ ounces) broccoli, chopped finely

1½ cups (180g) grated cheddar

1½ cups (150g) grated mozzarella

1 free-range egg, beaten lightly

3 teaspoons toasted sesame seeds

METHOD

1 Preheat oven to 200°C/400°F. Line two oven trays with baking paper.

2 Using a plate as a guide, cut six 22cm (8¾-inch) rounds from the pastry. Spread pastry with mustard, leaving a 1cm (½-inch) border around the edge.

3 Combine broccoli, cheddar and mozzarella in a large bowl; season. Place one-sixth of the broccoli mixture in centre of a pastry round; fold over to enclose filling, crimping the edge to seal. Repeat with remaining broccoli mixture and pastry rounds.

4 Place pies on trays. Brush with egg and sprinkle with seeds; cut four slashes on each pie.

5 Bake pies for 25 minutes or until golden and puffed.

TIP Pies can be made the day before up to the end of step 3; store, covered, in the fridge.

SERVES 6

PREP + COOK TIME 30 MINUTES

CARROT & LENTIL SOUP WITH CORIANDER PESTO

Lentils will thicken on standing; if necessary add a little extra water or stock to thin the soup. Serve with sourdough bread.

INGREDIENTS

2 tablespoons olive oil

1 large brown onion (200g), chopped coarsely

750g (1½ pounds) carrots, chopped coarsely

2 teaspoons ground cumin

2 teaspoons ground coriander

pinch dried chilli flakes

1 cup (200g) red lentils

1 litre (4 cups) vegetable stock

1½ cups (375ml) water

½ cup loosely packed fresh coriander (cilantro) leaves

CORIANDER PESTO

1 cup loosely packed fresh coriander (cilantro) leaves

1 small clove garlic, crushed

2 tablespoons roasted pistachios

¼ cup (60ml) olive oil

1 tablespoon lemon juice

METHOD

1 Heat oil in a large saucepan over medium heat; cook onion and carrot, covered, stirring occasionally, for 10 minutes or until softened. Add cumin, coriander and chilli; stir to coat. Add lentils and stock; bring to the boil. Reduce heat; simmer, covered, for 35 minutes or until lentils and carrots are soft. Cool soup for 10 minutes.

2 Meanwhile, make coriander pesto.

3 Blend or process soup until smooth. Return soup to pan with the water; bring to the boil. Season to taste. Serve soup drizzled with pesto and topped with coriander leaves.

CORIANDER PESTO Blend or process coriander, garlic and pistachios until finely chopped. With motor operating, add oil and juice in a thin, steady stream until combined. Season to taste.

SERVES 6

PREP + COOK TIME 50 MINUTES

EGGPLANT & PASTA POT PIES

These individual pot pies are perfect for winter, using eggplant and mushrooms to recreate the hearty flavour of traditional meat pies.

INGREDIENTS

1½ tablespoons olive oil

1 medium brown onion (150g), chopped finely

2 cloves garlic, crushed

1 medium eggplant (300g), peeled, chopped coarsely

200g (6½ ounces) swiss brown mushrooms, quartered

⅓ cup (80ml) red wine

2 tablespoons tomato paste

800g (1½ pounds) canned crushed tomatoes

¼ cup loosely packed fresh basil leaves, shredded finely

375g (12 ounces) penne pasta

1 free-range egg, beaten lightly

¾ cup (90g) coarsely grated cheddar

2 sheets frozen puff pastry, thawed

1 free-range egg white, beaten lightly

METHOD

1 Preheat oven to 200°C/400°F. Oil six 2-cup (500ml) ovenproof dishes.

2 Heat oil in a large saucepan over medium-high heat; cook onion and garlic, stirring, for 3 minutes or until onion is softened. Add eggplant and mushrooms; cook, stirring, for 5 minutes or until mushrooms begin to colour. Add wine; cook until nearly all the liquid is evaporated. Stir in paste and tomatoes; bring to the boil. Reduce heat; simmer, uncovered, for 15 minutes or until thickened. Stir in basil; season to taste.

3 Meanwhile, cook pasta in a large saucepan of boiling salted water until just tender; drain.

4 Place pasta and eggplant mixture in a large heatproof bowl with combined egg and cheddar; stir to combine.

5 Using one of the ovenproof dishes as a guide, cut six rounds, a little larger than the dish, from pastry.

6 Spoon pasta mixture into dishes. Brush edges of dishes with a little egg white. Top dishes with pastry rounds, pressing gently to seal. Brush lightly with a little more egg white. Place pies on an oven tray.

7 Bake pies for 15 minutes or until golden brown.

SERVING SUGGESTION Serve with a herb or green salad.

SERVES 6

PREP + COOK TIME 1 HOUR

CAULIFLOWER & TOFU RED CURRY

Serve curry immediately as tofu puffs will continue to absorb liquid on standing, or make curry 3 hours ahead; add tofu puffs on reheating.

INGREDIENTS

1 tablespoon peanut oil

1 medium brown onion (150g), sliced thinly

400ml can coconut milk (do not shake can) (see tips)

⅓ cup (100g) vegetarian red curry paste

2 teaspoons soy sauce

1 tablespoon lime juice

1 tablespoon light brown sugar

¾ cup (180ml) water

400g (12½ ounces) cauliflower, sliced thickly

250g (8 ounces) green beans, trimmed, halved lengthways

1 large zucchini (150g), sliced thickly

110g (3½ ounces) tofu puffs, cut in half diagonally

⅓ cup (25g) shaved fresh coconut (see tips), toasted lightly

⅓ cup loosely packed fresh coriander (cilantro)

1 fresh long red chilli, sliced thinly

1 medium lime (90g), cut into wedges

SERVES 4

PREP + COOK TIME 30 MINUTES

METHOD

1 Heat oil in a wok over medium heat; stir-fry onion for 2 minutes or until softened.

2 Add a spoonful of the solid coconut milk from the top of the can to wok. Add curry paste; cook, stirring, for 3 minutes or until oil separates and rises to the surface. Stir in soy sauce, juice, sugar, remaining coconut milk and the water; bring to the boil. Reduce heat to medium-low, add cauliflower to wok; simmer, covered, for 5 minutes. Add beans and zucchini; simmer, partially covered, for 5 minutes or until vegetables are tender. Add tofu; stir until hot. Season to taste.

3 Serve curry immediately topped with shaved coconut, coriander, chilli and lime wedges.

SERVING SUGGESTION Serve with steamed jasmine rice.

TIPS We used canned coconut milk that hasn't been emulsified, so it separates with the solid rising to the surface. If you have coconut milk that is emulsified, skip the step of adding the solids first.

Check curry paste label to ensure the paste doesn't contain any animal products.

To shave flesh from a fresh coconut, wrap the coconut in an old, clean tea towel and firmly hit the coconut on a hard floor, ideally outside and close to a bowl to catch the coconut water. Separate and discard the hard outer shell of the coconut. Use a vegetable peeler to shave the flesh.

If fresh coconut is not available, use moist coconut flakes instead.

MUSHROOM, CAVOLO NERO & QUINOA RISOTTO

Quinoa is gluten-free, a good source of protein, high in fibre, and – important for vegetarians – it contains all the essential amino acids.

INGREDIENTS

10g (½ ounce) dried porcini mushrooms

½ cup (125ml) boiling water

2 tablespoons olive oil

1 medium brown onion (150g), chopped finely

1 flat mushroom (80g), chopped coarsely

200g (6 ounces) swiss brown mushrooms, sliced thinly

2 cloves garlic, crushed

1 cup quinoa (200g), rinsed

1.25 litres (5 cups) vegetable stock

1 sprig fresh thyme

100g (3 ounces) cavolo nero (tuscan cabbage), sliced thinly

120g (4 ounces) goat's cheese, crumbled

⅓ cup (25g) finely grated parmesan

METHOD

1 Place porcini mushrooms in a heatproof bowl with the boiling water. Stand for 5 minutes.

2 Meanwhile, heat oil in a medium frying pan over medium heat; cook onion, stirring, for 3 minutes or until soft. Add flat and swiss brown mushrooms; cook, stirring, for 3 minutes or until browned and tender. Add garlic; cook, stirring, for 1 minute or until fragrant.

3 Stir in quinoa, stock and thyme. Remove porcini mushrooms from water (reserve the soaking liquid); chop coarsely. Add porcini and soaking liquid to pan; bring to the boil. Simmer, for 20 minutes until liquid is absorbed and quinoa is tender. Discard thyme. Add cavolo nero; stir until wilted. Remove pan from heat; stir in goat's cheese and half the parmesan.

4 Serve risotto topped with remaining parmesan. Season with freshly ground black pepper.

SERVING SUGGESTION Serve topped with a poached egg.

SERVES 4

PREP + COOK TIME 45 MINUTES

QUICHE PRIMAVERA

Quiche primavera encapsulates the taste of spring, using asparagus, green beans, peas and zucchini – all vegies at their peak in springtime.

INGREDIENTS

170g (5½ ounces) asparagus, trimmed, halved

60g (2 ounces) green beans, trimmed, halved lengthways

¼ cup (30g) frozen peas

1 small zucchini (90g), cut lengthways into ribbons

1 green onion (scallion), sliced thinly

4 free-range eggs

½ cup (125ml) pouring cream

½ cup (120g) sour cream

150g (4½ ounces) goat's cheese

¼ cup loosely packed small fresh mint leaves

SHORTCRUST PASTRY

1½ cups (225g) plain (all-purpose) flour

125g (4 ounces) cold butter, chopped coarsely

1 free-range egg yolk

2 tablespoons iced water, approximately

METHOD

1 Make shortcrust pastry.

2 Oil a 24cm (9½-inch) round loose-based flan tin. Roll pastry between sheets of baking paper until large enough to line tin. Lift pastry into tin; press into side, trim edge. Refrigerate for 20 minutes.

3 Preheat oven to 200°C/400°F.

4 Place flan tin on an oven tray; cover pastry with baking paper, fill with dried beans or rice. Bake for 10 minutes. Remove paper and beans; bake for 8 minutes or until browned lightly. Cool. Reduce oven to 180°C/350°F.

5 Meanwhile, boil, steam or microwave asparagus, beans and peas, separately, until just tender; drain. Refresh under cold water.

6 Arrange asparagus, beans, peas and zucchini in pastry case; sprinkle with green onion. Whisk eggs, cream and sour cream in a large jug; season. Pour over vegetables.

7 Bake quiche for 45 minutes or until just set. Serve topped with goat's cheese and mint leaves.

SHORTCRUST PASTRY Process flour and butter until crumbly. Add egg yolk and most of the water; process until ingredients just come together. Enclose in plastic wrap; refrigerate for 30 minutes.

TIPS Cover quiche with foil if it starts to overbrown during cooking. Pastry case can be baked to the end of step 4 a day ahead; store in an airtight container.

SERVES 6

PREP + COOK TIME 1 HOUR 45 MINUTES (+ REFRIGERATION)

SPINACH FLATBREADS & GREEK BEAN SALAD

Make spinach dough up to an hour ahead; cover and refrigerate until needed. Keep flatbread warm in a 120°C/250°F oven.

INGREDIENTS

250g (8 ounces) frozen chopped spinach, thawed

1 cup (150g) self-raising flour

½ cup (140g) greek-style yoghurt

1 clove garlic, crushed

2 tablespoons olive oil

200g (6½ ounces) tzatziki

1 medium lemon (140g), cut into wedges

GREEK BEAN SALAD

125g (4 ounces) medley cherry tomatoes, halved or quartered

1 lebanese cucumber (130g), chopped

½ cup (100g) canned cannellini beans, drained, rinsed

¼ cup (30g) pitted black olives, halved

¼ cup loosely packed fresh oregano leaves

100g (3 ounces) fetta, crumbled

METHOD

1 Place spinach in a clean tea towel. Squeeze over a sink to remove as much excess liquid as possible. Place spinach in a large bowl with flour, yoghurt and garlic; season. Use your hands to bring ingredients together and form a rough dough. Cover; stand for 1 hour.

2 Make greek bean salad.

3 Divide dough into eight balls. Roll out each ball of dough on a floured surface until 2mm (⅛ inch) thick.

4 Heat 1 teaspoon of the oil in a large frying pan over medium heat; cook one flatbread for 2 minutes each side or until golden. Remove from pan; cover to keep warm. Repeat with remaining oil and dough.

5 Top flatbreads with tzatziki and salad; serve with lemon wedges.

GREEK BEAN SALAD Place ingredients in a large bowl; toss gently to combine. Season to taste.

SERVES 4

PREP + COOK TIME 40 MINUTES (+ STANDING)

ASPARAGUS FRITTERS WITH HERB SALAD

You will need about 2 bunches of asparagus. If you can't find chardonnay vinegar, use a white wine vinegar or white balsamic vinegar.

INGREDIENTS

350g (11 ounces) asparagus, trimmed

1¼ cups (185g) self-raising flour

¾ cup (180ml) buttermilk

2 free-range eggs, beaten lightly

½ cup loosely packed fresh mint leaves, shredded finely

4 green onions (scallions), sliced thinly

¼ cup (60ml) vegetable oil

1 cup loosely packed fresh flat-leaf parsley leaves

1 cup loosely packed fresh coriander (cilantro) leaves

1 cup loosely packed fresh basil leaves

1 cup loosely packed fresh mint leaves, extra

2 tablespoons olive oil

1 tablespoon chardonnay vinegar

100g (3 ounces) smoked cheese, shaved

METHOD

1 Pour boiling water over asparagus in a medium heatproof bowl or dish; stand for 1 minute. Drain. Refresh in a bowl of iced water; drain. Cut asparagus into 1cm (½-inch) pieces.

2 Combine flour, buttermilk, egg, shredded mint, asparagus and half the green onion in a large bowl; season well.

3 Heat 1 tablespoon of the vegetable oil in a large non-stick frying pan over medium heat. Spoon 1 tablespoon of batter into pan; cook, in batches, for 1 minute each side or until fritters are browned and cooked through. Remove from pan; cover to keep warm.

4 Place herbs, olive oil, vinegar and remaining green onion in a medium bowl; toss gently to combine. Season to taste.

5 Serve fritters with salad and cheese.

SERVES 4 (MAKES 12 FRITTERS)

PREP + COOK TIME 30 MINUTES

RISOTTO-FILLED BAKED CAPSICUM

You can also use green capsicums in this recipe; they may take a little longer to soften than red and yellow varieties.

INGREDIENTS

40g (1½ ounces) butter

1 large brown onion (200g), chopped

2 cloves garlic, crushed

pinch saffron threads

1½ cups (300g) arborio rice

3 cups (750ml) vegetable stock

1 cup (250ml) water

1 cup (80g) finely grated parmesan

1 large zucchini (150g), grated coarsely

60g (2 ounces) baby spinach leaves

½ cup chopped fresh basil leaves

3 medium red capsicums
   (bell peppers) (600g)

3 medium yellow capsicums
   (bell peppers) (600g)

1 tablespoon olive oil

½ cup (125ml) water

METHOD

1 Preheat oven to 180°C/350°F.

2 Heat butter in a large heavy-based saucepan over medium-low heat; cook onion, stirring, for 10 minutes or until soft but not coloured. Add garlic, saffron and rice; cook, stirring, for 2 minutes or until fragrant. Add stock and the water; bring to the boil. Reduce heat to medium-low; cook, covered with tight-fitting lid, for 15 minutes or until almost tender and liquid is absorbed, stirring two or three times during cooking to check the rice is not sticking to the base of the pan. Remove from heat; stir in parmesan, zucchini, spinach and basil. Season to taste.

3 Meanwhile, cut tops from capsicums, about 1cm (½ inch) from the top; reserve tops with stalks intact. Remove seeds and membranes from capsicums; rinse, drain well. Rub half the oil over capsicums; season. Place capsicums in a small baking dish or ovenproof dish just large enough to hold the capsicums upright. Fill capsicums with rice mixture; replace tops. Drizzle capsicums with remaining oil; add the water to the dish.

4 Cover dish with lid or foil; bake for 40 minutes. Uncover, bake for a further 20 minutes or until capsicum are tender. Serve warm or at room temperature.

SERVES 6

PREP + COOK TIME 1 HOUR 45 MINUTES

CHEESY RISOTTO BALLS

To serve, use a mixture of herbs such as watercress, flat-leaf parsley, chervil, basil and chives. These would make a yummy entrée.

INGREDIENTS

40g (1½ ounces) butter

1 medium brown onion (150g), chopped finely

2 cloves garlic, crushed

2 cups (400g) arborio rice

½ cup (125ml) dry white wine

1 litre (4 cups) hot vegetable stock

½ cup (125ml) pouring cream

1 cup (80g) grated parmesan

½ cup (50g) grated mozzarella

2 free-range egg yolks

1½ cups (110g) panko (japanese) breadcrumbs

vegetable oil, for deep-frying

200g (6½ ounces) mixed olives

½ cup (150g) aïoli

1 cup loosely packed fresh mixed soft herbs (see note above)

1 medium lemon (140g), cut into wedges

METHOD

1 Heat butter in a medium saucepan over medium heat; cook onion and garlic, stirring, for 2 minutes or until onion is softened. Add rice, stir to coat in mixture. Add wine; cook, stirring, for 2 minutes or until wine has evaporated.

2 Gradually add hot stock, 1 cup at a time, stirring continuously, for 25 minutes or until all stock is used and rice is just cooked. Add cream; cook, stirring, for a further 2 minutes. Remove pan from heat, stir in parmesan and mozzarella. Cool for 20 minutes, then stir in egg yolks. Season. Spread rice mixture on a baking-paper-lined oven tray; cool for 15 minutes or until cool enough to handle.

3 With wet hands, gently roll slightly rounded tablespoons of the rice mixture into balls, then coat in breadcrumbs (the mixture will be quite delicate).

4 Fill a large saucepan one-third full with the oil; heat to 180°C/350°F (or until a cube of bread turns golden in 10 seconds). Fry risotto balls, in batches, for 2 minutes, turning occasionally, or until browned and heated through. Drain on paper towel.

5 Serve risotto balls immediately with olives, aïoli, herbs and lemon wedges.

TIP Risotto balls can be made to the end of step 3 up to 2 days ahead. Keep covered in the fridge.

MAKES ABOUT 50

PREP + COOK TIME 1 HOUR 15 MINUTES (+ COOLING)

THREE CHEESE RAVIOLI WITH BROWN BUTTER

Brown butter, known in French as beurre noisette, literally 'hazelnut butter', is an iconic part of traditional French cooking.

INGREDIENTS

12 zucchini flowers with stem attached (240g)

900g (1¾ pounds) three cheese ravioli

90g (3 ounces) butter, chopped

2 tablespoons fresh tarragon leaves

⅔ cup (90g) roasted hazelnuts, chopped coarsely

2 tablespoons lemon juice

METHOD

1 Discard yellow stamens from centre of flowers; trim stems. Cut zucchini flowers and attached stems in half lengthways.

2 Cook ravioli in a large saucepan of boiling salted water until just tender; remove ravioli with a slotted spoon. Bring water back to the boil, add zucchini flowers; boil for 5 seconds or until barely tender. Drain; add to ravioli.

3 Heat butter in a large frying pan until it begins to foam. Stir in tarragon; cook for 2 minutes or until butter begins to brown. Add hazelnuts, ravioli and zucchini flowers; toss until heated through. Add juice; toss to coat. Season to taste.

TIP You can use any vegetable- or cheese-filled ravioli you prefer.

SERVES 4

PREP + COOK TIME 25 MINUTES

OKONOMIYAKI WITH AVOCADO CREAM

Okonomiyaki is a Japanese savoury pancake containing a variety of ingredients; okonomi meaning "what you like" and yaki "to grill".

INGREDIENTS

¼ small cabbage (300g), sliced thinly

2 green onions (scallions), chopped finely

1 cup finely chopped fresh coriander (cilantro) leaves

5 free-range eggs, beaten lightly

1 cup (100g) packaged breadcrumbs

¼ cup (60ml) vegetable oil

1 tablespoon barbecue sauce

⅓ cup (90g) drained pickled ginger

2 teaspoons sesame seeds, toasted

AVOCADO CREAM

1 large avocado (320g), chopped

½ cup (150g) whole-egg mayonnaise

1 tablespoon lemon juice

METHOD

1 Combine cabbage, onion, coriander and egg in a large bowl. Stir in breadcrumbs; season. Stand for 10 minutes or until cabbage softens slightly.

2 Meanwhile, make avocado cream.

3 Heat 1 tablespoon of the oil in a large frying pan over medium heat; cook ⅓-cup measures of cabbage mixture, in batches, for 2 minutes each side, pressing with a spatula or until golden, firm and cooked through.

4 Serve okonomiyaki with avocado cream, barbecue sauce, ginger and sesame seeds.

AVOCADO CREAM Process avocado, mayonnaise and juice until smooth; season to taste.

TIP Cabbage mixture can be made up to 2 days ahead; store, covered, in the refrigerator.

SERVES 4

PREP + COOK TIME 40 MINUTES

CHICKPEA KOFTA WITH HARISSA YOGHURT

INGREDIENTS

2 corn cobs (800g), trimmed, husks and silks removed

¼ cup (60ml) olive oil

1 small brown onion (80g), chopped finely

3 teaspoons moroccan seasoning

800g (1½ pounds) canned chickpeas (garbanzo beans) drained, rinsed

1 free-range egg, beaten lightly

¼ cup (35g) plain (all-purpose) flour

¼ cup finely chopped fresh coriander (cilantro) leaves

¼ cup finely chopped fresh mint leaves

16 baby cos (romaine) lettuce leaves

1 lebanese cucumber (130g), peeled lengthways into ribbons

200g (6½ ounces) tomato medley, halved

HARISSA YOGHURT

1 cup (280g) greek-style yoghurt

2 teaspoons harissa paste

1 teaspoon honey

½ teaspoon ground cumin

METHOD

1 Brush corn with a little of the oil; season. Cook corn cobs on a heated oiled grill plate (or barbecue) over medium heat, turning occasionally, for 15 minutes or until charred and tender. When cool enough to handle, cut kernels from the cobs; place in a large bowl.

2 Meanwhile, preheat oven to 200°C/400°F.

3 Heat 2 teaspoons of the oil in a small frying pan over medium heat; cook onion, stirring occasionally, for 5 minutes or until soft. Add moroccan seasoning; cook, stirring, for 1 minute or until fragrant. Transfer mixture to bowl with corn; add chickpeas, then mash coarsely. Stir in egg, flour and herbs; season. Shape mixture into 16 koftas; place on a tray.

4 Heat remaining oil in same pan; cook kofta, in batches, over medium heat, turning occasionally, for 5 minutes or until golden. Transfer to an oven tray. Bake for 10 minutes or until cooked through.

5 Make harissa yoghurt.

6 Serve kofta in lettuce leaves with cucumber and tomato, drizzled with harissa yoghurt.

HARISSA YOGHURT Combine ingredients in a small bowl; season to taste.

TIPS Kofta can be made a day ahead; reheat, covered in foil, in the oven. You can use lebanese bread to wrap these up, with or without the lettuce.

SERVES 4

PREP + COOK TIME 45 MINUTES

FOUR WAYS WITH SEEDS

SEEDS & GRATED BEETROOT

Toast 2 tablespoons each pepitas (pumpkin seed kernels) and sunflower seeds in a dry frying pan. Place seeds in a medium bowl with 2 medium (350g) coarsely grated beetroot (beets), 200g (6½oz) crunchy sprouts combo, 2 tablespoons torn fresh mint leaves and 2 tablespoons each lemon juice and extra virgin olive oil; toss gently to combine. Season to taste.

SERVES 2

PREP + COOK TIME 15 MINUTES

SNACKING SEED MIX

Preheat oven to 180°C/350°F. Combine 2 tablespoons light brown sugar, 1 tablespoon tamari, 1 teaspoon ground cumin and ½ teaspoon each ground cinnamon and chilli flakes in a large bowl. Add 1 cup each pepitas (pumpkin seed kernels) and sunflower seeds, and 1 tablespoon each linseeds and white chia seeds; mix well. Spread seed mixture on baking-paper-lined oven tray. Bake for 20 minutes, turning and separating seeds until golden and roasted. Cool. Store in an airtight jar for up to 3 weeks.

MAKES 1¼ CUPS

PREP + COOK TIME 30 MINUTES

VEGIE SEED STICKS

Preheat oven to 220°C/425°F. Whisk 3 eggs in a shallow dish; season with pepper. Combine 2 cups (160g) finely grated parmesan and 2 tablespoons chia seeds on a large plate. Trim ends from 340g (11oz) asparagus. Cut 4 small (360g) zucchini lengthways into quarters. Working in batches, dip asparagus and zucchini into egg mixture; coat in cheese mixture. Place vegetables slightly apart between two baking-paper-lined oven trays. Roast for 15 minutes, swapping the trays, or until cheese is dark golden and vegetables are tender. Serve immediately sprinkled with salt flakes.

SERVES 4

PREP + COOK TIME 30 MINUTES

SEEDED FLATBREADS

Preheat oven to 190°C/375°F. Cut around the edge of three 20cm (8-inch) pitta breads; separate halves. Whisk ⅓ cup greek-style yoghurt and ⅓ cup extra virgin olive oil in a small bowl (don't worry if mixture looks separated). Combine 2 tablespoons crushed roasted hazelnuts, 2 teaspoons each nigella seeds and sesame seeds, 1 teaspoon each cumin seeds, crushed coriander seeds and flaked salt in a small bowl. Divide pitta halves between three oven trays (or bake in batches), brush with yoghurt mixture right up to the edge; scatter with seeds. Bake for 8 minutes or until golden. Cool. Serve with hummus.

SERVES 4

PREP + COOK TIME 30 MINUTES

POWER SALADS & SIDES

Ideas for plant-packed sides and filling salads, that are perfect for lunches, picnics and hot summer days. To eat as either a light meal on their own, or an accompaniment for a hearty main meal, these are yummy vegie dishes for all.

EGGPLANT, PROSCIUTTO & FETTA SALAD

Pomegranate molasses is thicker, browner, and more concentrated in flavour than it's juice – tart and sharp, slightly sweet and fruity.

INGREDIENTS

4 slices prosciutto (60g)

90g (3 ounces) sourdough bread, torn into pieces

2 tablespoons olive oil

8 lebanese eggplants (480g), cut into thirds lengthways

300g (9½ ounces) mixed baby tomatoes, halved

2 tablespoons small fresh basil leaves

2 tablespoons small fresh mint leaves

75g (2½ ounces) fetta, crumbled

POMEGRANATE DRESSING

1 small clove garlic, crushed

1 tablespoon pomegranate molasses

3 teaspoons sherry vinegar

¼ cup (60ml) olive oil

pinch dried chilli flakes

METHOD

1 Preheat oven to 200°C/400°F. Line two oven trays with baking paper.

2 Place prosciutto on one tray. Place bread on second tray; drizzle bread with half the oil. Bake prosciutto and bread for 15 minutes or until both are golden and crisp.

3 Meanwhile, drizzle eggplant with remaining oil; cook eggplant on a lightly oiled grill plate (or grill or barbecue), for 3 minutes each side or until golden and tender.

4 Make pomegranate dressing.

5 Combine eggplant, tomatoes, herbs and fetta on a platter; drizzle with dressing. Serve with prosciutto and bread.

POMEGRANATE DRESSING Place ingredients in a screw-top jar; shake well. Season to taste.

TIP Dressing can be made up to 4 days ahead; refrigerate in the jar.

SERVES 4

PREP + COOK TIME 35 MINUTES

VEG IT UP!

Skip the prosciutto and cook 1 large thickly sliced zucchini with the eggplant.

SUMAC EGGPLANT SKEWERS & CHILLI TOMATO SALAD

Sumac is a purple-red, astringent spice ground from berries growing on shrubs that flourish wild around the Mediterranean.

INGREDIENTS

2 large eggplants (1kg), chopped coarsely

2 medium lemons (280g), sliced thickly

2 tablespoons garlic oil

1 teaspoon ground sumac

2 tablespoons roasted flaked almonds

280g (9 ounces) labne

CHILLI TOMATO SALAD

400g (12½ ounces) mixed baby heirloom tomatoes, halved

1 tablespoon thinly sliced preserved lemon rind (see tip)

1 fresh long red chilli, seeded, sliced thinly

1 cup loosely packed fresh flat-leaf parsley leaves

½ cup loosely packed fresh mint leaves

2 tablespoons red wine vinegar

1 tablespoon garlic oil

METHOD

1 Place eggplant, lemon and oil in a medium bowl; toss to coat. Thread eggplant and lemon onto eight skewers; season.

2 Cook skewers on a heated oiled grill plate (or grill or barbecue) over medium-high heat for 3 minutes each side or until eggplant is browned and tender. Sprinkle with sumac.

3 Meanwhile, make chilli tomato salad.

4 Serve eggplant skewers on salad, sprinkled with almonds. Drizzle labne with a little extra oil and sumac, if desired; serve with skewers and salad.

CHILLI TOMATO SALAD Place all ingredients in a large bowl; stir gently to combine. Season to taste.

TIP Preserved lemon is available at delicatessens and some supermarkets. Remove and discard the flesh, rinse the rind well, then slice thinly. You could use 2 teaspoons finely grated lemon rind instead.

SERVES 4

PREP + COOK TIME 30 MINUTES

PEAR & WALNUT SALAD WITH TARRAGON PESTO

The sweet grilled fruit is contrasted with the crunch of the celery and fennel, and the richness of the blue cheese in this impressive salad.

INGREDIENTS

4 small corella pears (400g), sliced thickly crossways

2 stalks celery (300g), trimmed, sliced diagonally

1 cup firmly packed fresh celery leaves

1 baby fennel (130g), sliced very thinly

½ cup (50g) walnuts, roasted, chopped coarsely

100g (3 ounces) blue cheese, crumbled coarsely

TARRAGON PESTO

1 cup firmly packed fresh tarragon leaves

2 slices white bread (90g), crusts removed

¼ cup (60ml) milk

¼ cup (60ml) water

2 tablespoons olive oil

1 teaspoon sea salt

METHOD

1 Make tarragon pesto.

2 Cook pear on a heated oiled barbecue (or grill or grill pan) until browned lightly on both sides.

3 Place pear in a large bowl with celery and celery leaves, fennel and walnuts; mix gently to combine. Season to taste.

4 Serve salad topped pesto and blue cheese.

TARRAGON PESTO Blend or process ingredients until well combined; season to taste.

TIPS Use the yellow and lighter green leaves from the heart of the celery. Use a mandoline or V-slicer to cut the fennel into very thin slices.

SERVES 4

PREP + COOK TIME 30 MINUTES

PICKLED GREEN PAPAYA SALAD

Select a papaya that is very hard and slightly shiny for this recipe, which indicates it's fresh but not too unripe to grate or chop.

INGREDIENTS

1 cup (250ml) water

½ cup (125ml) rice vinegar

½ cup (110g) white (granulated) sugar

1 teaspoon sea salt

1 fresh long red chilli, halved lengthways

1 small green papaya (650g)
(see note above)

150g (4½ ounces) sugar snap peas, trimmed, halved lengthways

150g (4½ ounces) snow peas, trimmed, halved lengthways

100g (3 ounces) bean thread vermicelli

½ small pineapple (450g), quartered, chopped coarsely

1 small red onion (100g), sliced thinly

1 cup firmly packed fresh mint leaves

1 fresh long red chilli, extra, sliced thinly

PALM SUGAR DRESSING

¼ cup (60ml) lime juice

2 tablespoons grated palm sugar

METHOD

1 Stir the water, vinegar, sugar, salt and halved chilli in a small saucepan; bring to the boil. Reduce heat; simmer, uncovered, for 5 minutes. Strain into a small jug; discard solids. Cool 10 minutes.

2 Meanwhile, peel papaya. Quarter lengthways, discard seeds. Cut papaya into long thin matchsticks.

3 Place papaya in a medium bowl the with vinegar mixture. Cover; stand for 1 hour. Drain; discard liquid.

4 Boil, steam or microwave peas until just tender; drain.

5 Place noodles in a medium heatproof bowl, with enough boiling water to cover. Stand until just tender; drain. Rinse under cold water; drain. Using kitchen scissors, cut noodles into random lengths.

6 Make palm sugar dressing.

7 Place papaya, peas and noodles in a medium bowl with pineapple, onion, mint and dressing; toss gently to combine.

8 Divide salad between bowls; top with extra sliced chilli.

PALM SUGAR DRESSING Place ingredients in a screw-top jar; shake well. Season to taste.

TIP Green (unripe) papayas are readily available in various sizes at many greengrocers, Asian food shops and markets.

SERVES 4

PREP + COOK TIME 30 MINUTES (+ STANDING)

STEAMED ASIAN GREENS WITH TOFU

Soaking up the flavours from sauces, soups and spices, tofu is a great substitute for meat or fish, being both high in calcium and iron.

INGREDIENTS

600g (1¼ pounds) soft silken tofu

1 tablespoon sesame oil

⅓ cup (80ml) vegetarian oyster sauce (see tips)

350g (11 ounces) broccolini, chopped coarsely

4 baby buk choy (600g), halved lengthways

170g (5½ ounces) asparagus, trimmed, halved

1 medium red onion (170g), chopped finely

1 fresh long red chilli, sliced thinly

PALM SUGAR DRESSING

⅓ cup (80ml) lime juice

1 tablespoon grated palm sugar

1 tablespoon soy sauce

METHOD

1 Pat tofu dry with paper towel; chop coarsely. Place tofu, in a single layer, on a paper-towel-lined tray. Stand for 30 minutes.

2 Heat 3 teaspoons of the oil in a wok over high heat; stir-fry tofu until all liquid has been absorbed and tofu has browned lightly. Stir in oyster sauce. Remove from wok; cover to keep warm.

3 Meanwhile, boil, steam or microwave broccolini, buk choy and asparagus, separately, until tender; drain.

4 Make palm sugar dressing.

5 Divide asian greens between plates; drizzle with dressing. Top with tofu mixture, red onion and chilli.

PALM SUGAR DRESSING Place ingredients in a screw-top jar; shake well.

TIPS While regular oyster sauce is made from oysters and their brine, vegetarian oyster sauce is made from mushrooms (most often oyster or shiitake mushrooms).

Palm sugar dressing can be made 2 days ahead; refrigerate in the jar.

SERVES 4

PREP + COOK TIME 1 HOUR (+ STANDING)

TIPS You need to start this recipe
a day ahead. If you don't have time to
make your own labne, you can use 3 cups
(840g) store-bought labne.

Use mixed salad leaves if no beetroot
leaves are available. The dressing can be
made 1 week ahead; refrigerate in the jar.

Add herbs and leaves to the salad just
before serving, to prevent discolouring.

LENTIL, BEETROOT & LABNE SALAD

INGREDIENTS

You will need to start this recipe 24 hours ahead.

1kg (2 pounds) greek-style yoghurt

500g (1 pound) baby beetroot (beets), trimmed, small leaves reserved

500g (1 pound) golden baby beetroot (beets), trimmed, small leaves reserved

2 tablespoons olive oil

1 cup (200g) french-style green lentils

120g (4 ounces) baby spinach leaves

2 tablespoons lemon juice

¼ cup (60ml) olive oil, extra

150g (4½ ounces) baby green beans, trimmed

½ cup loosely packed fresh baby basil leaves

½ cup loosely packed fresh flat-leaf parsley leaves

½ cup loosely packed fresh chervil leaves

½ cup chopped fresh chives

DRESSING

2 tablespoons olive oil

2 tablespoons red wine vinegar

1 teaspoon sugar

SERVES 6

PREP + COOK TIME 1 HOUR 15 MINUTES (+ REFRIGERATION)

METHOD

1 To make the labne, line a large sieve with two layers of muslin or cheesecloth; place sieve over a deep bowl or jug large enough to hold sieve. Spoon yoghurt into sieve, gather cloth and tie into a ball with kitchen string. Hang above bowl. Refrigerate for 24 hours or until thick, gently squeezing occasionally to encourage the liquid to drain. Discard liquid. Transfer labne to a large bowl.

2 Preheat oven to 180°C/350°F.

3 Trim beetroot; reserve 100g (3 ounces) of the nicest, smallest beetroot leaves. Wash beetroot well. Place in a roasting pan; drizzle with oil. Cover pan with foil; roast for 45 minutes or until tender. Stand for 10 minutes. When cool enough to handle, remove skins (they should slip off easily; if not use a small knife). Cut beetroot in half or quarters.

4 Meanwhile, cook lentils in a medium saucepan of boiling water, uncovered, for 12 minutes or until tender; drain. Rinse under cold water; drain well.

5 Blend or process spinach, juice and extra oil until well combined; season to taste.

6 Pour boiling water over beans in a large heatproof bowl; stand for 1 minute. Drain. Refresh beans in another bowl of iced water; drain well.

7 Make dressing.

8 Place beetroot, lentils and beans in a large bowl with herbs, reserved beetroot leaves and half the dressing; toss to combine.

9 Spread labne on a platter; top with spinach mixture and salad. Drizzle with remaining dressing.

DRESSING Place ingredients in a screw-top jar; shake well. Season.

PUMPKIN, BASIL & CHILLI STIR-FRY

This stir-fry uses traditional South-East Asian flavours to spice up pumpkin, a vegetable usually baked. Serve with basmati or brown rice.

INGREDIENTS

⅓ cup (80ml) peanut oil

¾ cup loosely packed fresh thai basil leaves

2 cloves garlic, sliced thinly

4 fresh small red thai chillies, sliced thinly

1kg (2 pounds) jap pumpkin, sliced thickly

1 large red onion (300g), cut into thin wedges

250g (8 ounces) sugar snap peas, trimmed

1 teaspoon grated palm sugar

¼ cup (60ml) vegetable stock

2 tablespoons soy sauce

4 green onions (scallions), sliced thinly

½ cup (75g) roasted unsalted peanuts

METHOD

1 Heat oil in a wok over high heat; cook half the basil for 1 minute or until crisp but still green. Remove with a slotted spoon; drain on paper towel.

2 Stir-fry garlic and chilli in wok for 1 minute or until fragrant. Add pumpkin and onion; stir-fry for 8 minutes or until browned all over and just tender. Add peas, sugar, stock and soy sauce; stir-fry until sauce thickens slightly.

3 Remove wok from heat. Add green onion, peanuts and remaining basil; toss until well combined. Serve topped with crisp basil.

TIP To help reduce the heat in this stir-fry, you can reduce the number of chillies or remove the seeds and membranes. Or, use large chillies rather than small as they are not as hot.

SERVES 4

PREP + COOK TIME 25 MINUTES

CRISPY THAI TOFU WITH POMELO SLAW

Tofu can be marinated a day ahead; keep covered in the fridge.
You can use grapefruit instead of pomelo, if you prefer.

INGREDIENTS

600g (1¼ pounds) hard tofu,
  cut into 8 slices

2 fresh long red chillies, seeded

10cm (4-inch) stick fresh lemon grass
  (20g), white part only, chopped finely

¼ cup (60ml) olive oil

½ pomelo (340g), segmented (see tips)

¼ medium cabbage (375g), sliced thinly

1 medium carrot (120g), cut into
  long thin strips (see tips)

1 small red onion (100g), sliced thinly

1 cup loosely packed fresh coriander
  (cilantro) leaves, chopped coarsely

½ cup (70g) roasted peanuts,
  chopped coarsely

GINGER DRESSING

¼ cup (60ml) pomelo juice

1 tablespoon lime juice

2 tablespoons olive oil

1 tablespoon light soy sauce

1 tablespoon finely grated fresh ginger

2 teaspoons caster (superfine) sugar

METHOD

1 Pat tofu dry with paper towel. Finely chop 1 chilli; thinly slice other chilli. Combine lemon grass, chopped chilli and oil in a large shallow dish. Add tofu; turn to coat. Stand for at least 10 minutes.

2 Meanwhile, make ginger dressing; reserve ⅓ cup.

3 Place pomelo segments, cabbage, carrot, onion, coriander and sliced chilli in a large bowl with remaining dressing; toss gently to combine. Sprinkle with peanuts.

4 Cook tofu, in batches, on a heated oiled grill plate (or grill or barbecue) over high heat for 3 minutes each side or until golden and crisp. Drain on paper towel.

5 Divide slaw between bowls. Serve topped with tofu slices, drizzled with reserved dressing.

GINGER DRESSING Combine ingredients in a small bowl. Season.

TIPS To segment the pomelo, cut the top and bottom from pomelo; cut off the rind with the white pith, following the curve of the fruit. Cut down either side of each segment close to the membrane to release each segment. Use a julienne peeler to cut the carrot into long thin strips. Julienne peelers are available from kitchenware stores and Asian food stores.

SERVES 4

PREP + COOK TIME 25 MINUTES

FIVE-GRAIN SALAD

The salad can be prepared ahead of time; add dressing just before serving. Omit the goat's fetta to make it vegan.

INGREDIENTS

⅓ cup (70g) black quinoa, rinsed

⅔ cup (160ml) cold water

⅓ cup (65g) couscous

⅓ cup (80ml) boiling water

⅓ cup (65g) barley

⅓ cup (65g) wholegrain greenwheat freekeh

⅓ cup (65g) brown rice

3 medium oranges (720g)

1 medium red apple (150g), unpeeled, sliced thinly

1 small red onion (100g), sliced thinly

1 cup loosely packed fresh flat-leaf parsley leaves

½ cup loosely packed fresh mint leaves

⅓ cup (80ml) olive oil

200g (6½ ounces) goat's fetta, crumbled

½ cup (80g) brazil nuts, chopped coarsely

METHOD

1 Place quinoa and the cold water in a small saucepan; bring to the boil. Reduce heat to low; simmer, uncovered, for 15 minutes, stirring occasionally, or until most of the water is absorbed. Remove from heat; cover, stand for 5 minutes.

2 Meanwhile, combine couscous with the boiling water in a large heatproof bowl. Cover; stand for 5 minutes or until liquid is absorbed, fluffing with fork occasionally.

3 Cook barley, freekeh and rice in a large saucepan of boiling water for 25 minutes or until tender. Drain; rinse under cold water, drain well.

4 Remove rind from oranges with a zester (see tip). Cut the top and bottom from each orange. Cut off the white pith, following the curve of the fruit. Hold fruit over a bowl to catch the juices; cut down both sides of the white membrane to release each segment. Reserve juice.

5 Place all grains, rind and orange segments in a large bowl with apple, onion and herbs; toss to combine. Season to taste.

6 To make dressing, place oil and 2 tablespoons of the reserved juice in a screw-top jar; shake well. Season to taste.

7 Add dressing to salad with half the fetta; toss gently to combine. Serve salad on a platter topped with brazil nuts and remaining fetta.

TIP If you don't have a zester to create thin strips of orange rind, use a vegetable peeler to peel long, wide pieces of rind from the oranges, without the white pith, then cut them lengthways into thin strips.

SERVES 6

PREP + COOK TIME 45 MINUTES

WARM SPINACH & POTATO SALAD

Using very fresh free-range or organic eggs will give the best results.
The dressing can be made 2 days ahead; refrigerate in the jar.

INGREDIENTS

500g (1 pound) kipfler (fingerling)
  potatoes, scrubbed

2 tablespoons olive oil

1 teaspoon white vinegar

4 free-range eggs (see notes above)

250g (8 ounces) haloumi,
  cut into 5mm (¼-inch) slices

200g (6½ ounces) baby spinach leaves

MUSTARD DRESSING

2 tablespoons olive oil

2 tablespoons white balsamic vinegar

1 tablespoon dijon mustard

1 shallot (25g), chopped finely

1 tablespoon honey

METHOD

1 Boil, steam or microwave potatoes until just tender; drain.
Cut potatoes in half.

2 Heat oil in a large non-stick frying pan over medium heat; cook
potatoes for 10 minutes, turning occasionally, or until golden brown
and tender. Season. Remove potatoes with a slotted spoon; drain
on paper towel. Cover to keep warm. Reserve oil in pan.

3 Meanwhile, make mustard dressing.

4 Half-fill a large deep frying pan with water; bring to the boil,
add white vinegar. Break one egg into a cup. Stir the water to
make a small whirlpool then gently slide the egg into centre of
whirlpool; repeat with remaining eggs. Return water to the boil.
Cover pan, turn off heat; stand for 4 minutes or until a light film
of egg white sets over yolks. Remove eggs, one at a time, using a
slotted spoon; drain on paper towel. Cover to keep warm.

5 Meanwhile, heat reserved oil in frying pan over medium-high
heat; cook haloumi, on both sides, until golden brown. Drain on
paper towel. Pour half the dressing into pan; turn off heat.

6 Place potatoes and haloumi in a large bowl with spinach and
remaining dressing; toss gently to combine. Serve topped with
eggs, drizzled with warm dressing. Season. Serve immediately.

MUSTARD DRESSING Place ingredients in a screw-top jar; shake
well. Season to taste.

SERVES 4

PREP + COOK TIME 30 MINUTES

SMOKY EGGPLANT SALAD WITH TAHINI

This recipe is perfect for a picnic. Transport eggplant salad and yoghurt sauce separately. Assemble salad just before serving.

INGREDIENTS

1 small red onion (100g), halved, sliced very thinly

2 tablespoons lemon juice

5 medium eggplant (1.5kg)

1½ tablespoons tahini

2 cloves garlic, crushed

1 cup (280g) greek-style yoghurt

2 tablespoons extra virgin olive oil

1 cup loosely packed fresh mint leaves, torn

1 teaspoon ground sumac

METHOD

1 Combine onion and half the juice in a small bowl.

2 Preheat a barbecue (or grill plate) over high heat. Prick eggplants all over with a fork. Cook eggplants on heated barbecue, turning occasionally, for 30 minutes or until skin is charred and flesh is very tender. Place eggplant in a large sieve over a large bowl; drain. Cool.

3 Meanwhile, combine tahini, garlic, yoghurt and remaining juice in a small bowl. Season to taste.

4 Remove and discard skin from eggplant; using two forks, pull apart the flesh into pieces. Spoon eggplant onto a large platter; season well, then drizzle with oil.

5 Serve topped with onion mixture, mint and yoghurt sauce. Sprinkle with sumac.

SERVES 8 AS A SIDE

PREP + COOK TIME 45 MINUTES

SESAME OMELETTE & VEGETABLE SALAD

To transport, store the salad mixture, omelette and dressing separately; add the omelette and dress the salad just before serving.

INGREDIENTS

8 free-range eggs

½ cup (125ml) milk

½ cup coarsely chopped fresh garlic chives

2 tablespoons toasted sesame seeds

8 cups (640g) finely shredded wombok (napa cabbage)

1 large red capsicum (bell pepper) (350g), sliced thinly

1 large green capsicum (bell pepper) (350g), sliced thinly

1 tablespoon coarsely chopped fresh mint leaves

5cm (2-inch) stick fresh lemon grass (10g), white part only, chopped finely

2 fresh long red chillies, sliced thinly

SWEET CHILLI DRESSING

¼ cup (60ml) rice vinegar

¼ cup (60ml) peanut oil

¼ cup (60ml) sweet chilli sauce

1 teaspoon sesame oil

2 teaspoons toasted sesame seeds

METHOD

1 Whisk eggs in a large jug with milk, chives and seeds until well combined. Pour a quarter of the egg mixture into a heated lightly oiled wok; cook over medium heat, tilting pan, until omelette is just set. Remove from wok. Repeat with remaining egg mixture to make four omelettes in total. Cool. Roll omelettes tightly; cut into thin slices.

2 Make sweet chilli dressing.

3 Place three-quarters of the omelette in a large bowl with wombok, capsicums, mint, lemon grass, dressing and half the chilli; toss gently to combine.

4 Serve salad topped with remaining omelette and chilli.

SWEET CHILLI DRESSING Place ingredients in a screw-top jar; shake well. Season to taste.

TIPS You will need about half a medium wombok for this recipe.

Omelettes can be made up to 3 hours ahead and stored, covered, in the refrigerator; roll and slice just before assembling salad.

SERVES 4

PREP + COOK TIME 35 MINUTES

CHAR-GRILLED VEGETABLE COUSCOUS

Use drained purchased char-grilled vegetables if you are short on time.
Serve topped with crumbled fetta or goat's cheese, if you like.

INGREDIENTS

1 medium red capsicum (bell pepper)
(200g), quartered

4 baby eggplant (240g),
sliced thinly lengthways

1 large zucchini (150g),
sliced thinly lengthways

1½ tablespoons olive oil

1 cup (250ml) vegetable stock

1 cup (200g) couscous

⅓ cup (80ml) olive oil

2 tablespoons red wine vinegar

1 teaspoon caster (superfine) sugar

⅓ cup (55g) dried currants

½ cup (60g) pitted kalamata olives

⅓ cup (50g) pine nuts, roasted

¼ cup loosely packed fresh mint leaves

¼ cup loosely packed fresh coriander
(cilantro) leaves

¼ cup (40g) pomegranate seeds

METHOD

1 Place capsicum, eggplant, zucchini and oil in a large bowl;
toss to coat vegetables in oil. Season.

2 Cook vegetables, in batches, on a heated oiled grill plate
(or grill or barbecue) over medium-high heat until tender.
Cut capsicum into thick slices.

3 Bring stock to the boil in a medium saucepan. Remove pan
from heat; stir in couscous and 2 teaspoons of the oil. Cover;
stand for 5 minutes or until liquid is absorbed, fluffing with
a fork occasionally.

4 Place vinegar, sugar, currants and remaining oil in a screw-top
jar; shake well. Season to taste.

5 Place vegetables and couscous in a large bowl with olives,
pine nuts and dressing; toss gently to combine. Serve topped
with herbs and pomegranate seeds.

TIP   Make the dressing several hours ahead to let the currant become plump.

SERVES 4

PREP + COOK TIME 30 MINUTES

ZUCCHINI & SWEET POTATO LOAF

Use butternut pumpkin or carrot instead of the sweet potato, if you like. Spread with butter or herb-flavoured soft cheese or goat's cheese.

INGREDIENTS

1 tablespoon olive oil

1 medium brown onion (150g), chopped finely

2 cloves garlic, crushed

2 teaspoons finely chopped fresh rosemary

2 large zucchini (300g), grated coarsely

1 small white sweet potato (250g), grated coarsely

1 cup (150g) self-raising flour

1 cup (80g) finely grated parmesan

½ teaspoon ground nutmeg

1 teaspoon cracked black pepper

5 free-range eggs, beaten lightly

½ cup (125ml) buttermilk

¼ cup (35g) drained sun-dried tomatoes in oil, sliced thinly

1 long sprig fresh rosemary

METHOD

1 Preheat oven to 180°C/350°F. Grease a 10cm x 20cm (4-inch x 8-inch) loaf pan (top measurement); line base and long sides with baking paper, extending the paper 5cm (2 inches) over the edges.

2 Heat oil in a medium frying pan over medium heat; cook onion, garlic and chopped rosemary, stirring, for 4 minutes or until lightly golden. Transfer to a large bowl; cool slightly.

3 Squeeze excess liquid from zucchini. Add zucchini to onion mixture with sweet potato, flour, parmesan, nutmeg and pepper; mix to combine. Make a well in the centre, add egg, buttermilk and tomatoes; mix until just combined. Spread mixture into pan; top with rosemary sprig.

4 Bake loaf for 1 hour or until browned and a skewer inserted into the centre comes out clean. Cover loosely with foil if overbrowning during cooking. Cool in pan for 20 minutes before turning out.

5 Serve sliced, warm or at room temperature.

TIP If you can't find buttermilk, you can make your own: place 2 teaspoons lemon juice in a jug and add enough low-fat milk to make up to ½ cup (125ml).

SERVES 6

PREP + COOK TIME 1 HOUR 20 MINUTES (+ COOLING)

QUINOA, KALE & CORIANDER SALAD

Cauliflower is also delicious roasted in the same way as
the broccolini; allow about an extra 10 minutes cooking time.

INGREDIENTS

1 cup (200g) tri-colour quinoa

2 cups (500ml) water

450g (14½ ounces) broccolini, trimmed,
halved crossways

280g (9 ounces) kale, stalks removed,
torn coarsely

¼ cup (50g) pepitas (pumpkin seed
kernels)

⅓ cup (55g) coarsely chopped
smoked almonds

2 fresh long green chillies, seeded,
sliced thinly

3 cloves garlic, chopped

¼ cup (60ml) extra virgin olive oil

1 large avocado (320g), chopped

CORIANDER LIME DRESSING

1 cup loosely packed fresh coriander
(cilantro) leaves

1 fresh long green chilli, seeded, chopped

¼ cup (60ml) olive oil

2 tablespoons lime juice

METHOD

1 Preheat oven to 220°C/425°F.

2 Place quinoa and the water in a medium saucepan; bring to the boil. Reduce heat to low; simmer, covered, for 10 minutes or until tender. Rinse under cold water; drain well. Transfer to a large bowl.

3 Combine broccolini, kale, pepitas, almonds, chilli, garlic and oil in a large shallow baking dish or oven trays; season. Roast for 8 minutes or until broccolini is tender and kale is wilted, stirring twice during cooking.

4 Meanwhile, make coriander lime dressing.

5 Add kale mixture to quinoa; mix gently to combine.

6 Serve salad topped with avocado, drizzled with dressing.

CORIANDER LIME DRESSING Place ingredients in a blender or food processor; pulse until finely chopped. Season to taste.

TIP Squeeze a little extra lime juice over the avocado to prevent browning if you are packaging and transporting the salad.

SERVES 4

PREP + COOK TIME 40 MINUTES

PUMPKIN POLENTA WEDGES WITH ROMESCO

Romesco is a nut and red capsicum-based sauce that originated from Northeastern Spain; it would also be delicious with fish or chicken.

INGREDIENTS

500g (1 pound) butternut pumpkin, peeled, cut into 1cm (½-inch) pieces

2 cups (500ml) milk

2 cups (500ml) vegetable stock or water

1 cup (170g) instant polenta

¾ cup (60g) finely grated parmesan

400g (12½ ounces) canned white beans, drained, rinsed

2 tablespoons olive oil

60g (2 ounces) baby rocket (arugula) leaves

90g (3 ounces) soft goat's cheese, crumbled

ROMESCO

½ cup (100g) drained char-grilled red capsicum (bell pepper) strips

¼ cup (40g) natural almonds

2 tablespoons olive oil

1 tablespoon red wine vinegar

½ clove garlic, crushed

½ teaspoon smoked paprika

METHOD

1 Boil, steam or microwave pumpkin until tender; drain.

2 Grease a 20cm x 30cm (8-inch x 12-inch) slice pan; line base and long sides with baking paper, extending the paper by 5cm (2 inches) above the edges.

3 Place milk and stock in a large saucepan over medium heat; bring to a simmer. Gradually add polenta, stirring constantly. Reduce heat to low; cook, stirring, for 10 minutes or until polenta thickens. Stir in parmesan, pumpkin and beans; season to taste. Spread polenta mixture into pan; cool for 10 minutes. Cover; refrigerate for 2 hours or until firm.

4 Preheat oven to 220°C/400°F.

5 Cut polenta into wedges; place wedges on a baking-paper-lined oven tray, drizzle with oil. Bake for 25 minutes, turning once, or until golden and crisp.

6 Meanwhile, make romesco.

7 Serve polenta with rocket, goat's cheese and romesco.

ROMESCO Blend or process ingredients until smooth. Season.

TIP Polenta can be made, to the end of step 3, up to 2 days ahead.

SERVES 4

PREP + COOK TIME 50 MINUTES (+ REFRIGERATION)

FOUR WAYS WITH FENNEL

HONEY-ROASTED FENNEL

Preheat oven to 200°C/400°F. Reserve ¼ cup green fennel fronds from 4 baby (520g) fennel bulbs. Cut fennel bulbs in half; place on a baking-paper-lined oven tray. Add 8 fresh thyme sprigs and 2 tablespoons each honey and olive oil; mix to combine. Turn fennel cut-side down; season. Roast for 25 minutes or until tender and browned. Serve fennel drizzled with balsamic vinegar, topped with reserved fronds and ¼ cup roasted flaked almonds.

SERVES 4

PREP + COOK TIME 35 MINUTES

GRAPEFRUIT FENNEL SALAD

Cut 1 pink grapefruit (350g) into segments. Place grapefruit in a medium bowl with 1 medium (300g) thinly shaved fennel bulb and ¼ cup squashed sicilian olives; toss gently to combine. Whisk ¼ cup grapefruit juice, 1 crushed clove garlic, 1½ tablespoons sherry vinegar and 2 tablespoons olive oil in a small bowl. Serve drizzled with dressing.

SERVES 4

PREP TIME 15 MINUTES

TIP Use the drained marinating oil from the persian fetta to brush on the bread before char-grilling.

FENNEL

SHAVED FENNEL SLAW

Place 350g (11oz) shredded white cabbage in a large bowl with 1 medium (300g) thinly shaved fennel bulb, 1 thinly sliced seeded green chilli, 1 cup each fresh coriander (cilantro) and fresh mint leaves; toss gently to combine. Combine ¼ cup each lemon juice and extra virgin olive oil in a small bowl; season to taste. Drizzle dressing over slaw; toss gently to combine.

SERVES 4

PREP TIME 15 MINUTES

FENNEL BRUSCHETTA

Place 1 small (200g) thinly sliced fennel bulb in a medium bowl with 1 crushed clove garlic, ⅓ cup white balsamic vinegar, 2 teaspoons caster (superfine) sugar and 6 thinly sliced red radishes; toss to combine. Stand for 30 minutes. Drain. Spread 180g (5½oz) drained persian fetta on 4 slices char-grilled sourdough bread; top with pickled fennel.

SERVES 4

PREP + COOK TIME 15 MINUTES (+ STANDING)

GLOSSARY

ALMONDS
flat, pointy-tipped nuts with a pitted brown shell enclosing a creamy white kernel which is covered by a brown skin. **flaked** paper-thin slices.

BARLEY a nutritious grain used in soups and stews. Hulled barley, the least processed, is high in fibre.

BEANS
cannellini small white bean similar in appearance and flavour to haricot, great northern and navy beans, all of which can be substituted for the other. **green** also known as french or string beans (although the tough string they once had has generally been bred out of them), this long thin fresh bean is consumed in its entirety once cooked.

BEETROOT (BEETS) also known as red beets; firm, round root vegetable.

BREADCRUMBS
packaged prepared fine-textured but crunchy white breadcrumbs; good for coating foods that are to be fried. **panko (japanese)** available in two kinds: larger pieces and fine crumbs; have a lighter texture than Western-style ones.
stale crumbs made by grating, blending or processing 1- or 2-day-old bread.

BUCKWHEAT a herb in the same plant family as rhubarb; not a cereal so it is gluten-free. Available as flour; ground (cracked) into coarse, medium or fine granules (kasha) and used similarly to polenta; or groats, the whole kernel sold roasted as a cereal product.

BUK CHOY also called bok choy, pak choi, chinese white cabbage or chinese chard; has a fresh, mild mustard taste.

BUTTERMILK originally the term given to the slightly sour liquid left after butter was churned from cream, today it is made from no-fat or low-fat milk to which specific bacterial cultures have been added. Despite its name, it is actually low in fat.

CHEESE
blue mould-treated cheeses mottled with blue veining.
cheddar the most common cow's milk 'tasty' cheese; should be aged, hard and have a pronounced bite.
fetta Greek in origin; a crumbly textured goat- or sheep-milk cheese having a sharp, salty taste.
fetta, persian a soft, creamy fetta marinated in a blend of olive oil, garlic, herbs and spices; available from most major supermarkets.
goat's made from goat's milk, has an earthy, strong taste. Available in soft, crumbly and firm textures, in various shapes and sizes, and sometimes rolled in ash or herbs.
haloumi a Greek Cypriot cheese with a semi-firm, spongy texture and very salty sweet flavour. Ripened and stored in salted whey; best grilled or fried, it holds its shape well on being heated. Eat while still warm as it becomes tough and rubbery on cooling.
mozzarella soft, spun-curd cheese originating in southern Italy where it was traditionally made from water-buffalo milk. Now generally made from cow's milk, it is the most popular pizza cheese because of its low melting point and elasticity when heated.
parmesan also called parmigiano; a hard, grainy cow-milk cheese originating in Italy.
pecorino the Italian generic name for cheeses made from sheep's milk. If you can't find it, use parmesan.

CHIA SEEDS contain protein and all the essential amino acids and a wealth of vitamins, minerals and antioxidants, as well as being fibre-rich.

CHICKPEAS (GARBANZO BEANS) an irregularly round, sandy-coloured legume. Has a firm texture even after cooking, a floury mouth-feel and robust nutty flavour; available canned or dried.

CHILLI
available in many types and sizes. Removing membranes and seeds lessens the heat level.
flakes dried, deep-red, dehydrated chilli slices and whole seeds.
jalapeño pronounced hah-lah-pain-yo. Fairly hot, medium-sized, plump, dark green chilli; available pickled, sold canned or bottled, and fresh, from greengrocers.
long green any unripened chilli.
long red available both fresh and dried; a generic term used for any moderately hot, thin, long chilli.
thai (serrano) also known as 'scuds'; tiny, very hot and bright red in colour.

COCONUT
flaked dried flaked coconut flesh.
milk not the liquid found inside the fruit (coconut water), but the diluted liquid from the second pressing of the white flesh of a mature coconut (the first pressing produces coconut cream). Available in cans and cartons at most supermarkets.
oil is extracted from the coconut flesh so you don't get any of the fibre, protein or carbohydrates present in the whole coconut. The best quality is virgin coconut oil, which is the oil pressed from the dried coconut flesh, and doesn't include the use of solvents or other refining processes.

CORIANDER (CILANTRO) also called pak chee or chinese parsley; bright-green-leafed herb with a pungent flavour. The leaves, stems and roots of coriander are also used. Also available ground or as seeds; these should not be substituted for fresh coriander.

COUSCOUS a fine, grain-like cereal product made from semolina; from the countries of North Africa. A semolina flour and water dough is sieved then dehydrated to produce minuscule even-sized pellets of couscous; it is rehydrated by steaming or with the addition of a warm liquid and swells to three or four times its original size; eaten like rice with a tagine.

CREAM
pouring also known as pure or fresh cream. It has no additives and contains a minimum fat content of 35%.
sour a thick, commercially-cultured sour cream with a minimum fat content of 35%.

EGGPLANT also known as aubergine. Ranging in size from tiny to very large and in colour from pale green to deep purple.

FENNEL also called finocchio or anise; a crunchy green vegetable slightly resembling celery that's eaten raw in salads; fried as an accompaniment; or used as an ingredient in soups and sauces. Also the name given to the dried seeds of the plant which have a stronger licorice flavour.

FLOUR
plain (all-purpose) unbleached wheat flour, the best for baking: the gluten content ensures a strong dough, for a light result.

rice very fine, almost powdery, gluten-free flour; made from ground white rice. Used in baking, as a thickener, and in some Asian noodles and desserts. Another variety, made from glutinous sweet rice, is used for chinese dumplings and rice paper.
self-raising all-purpose plain or wholemeal flour with baking powder and salt added; make at home in the proportion of 1 cup plain or wholemeal flour to 2 teaspoons baking powder.

FREEKEH is cracked roasted green wheat and can be found in some larger supermarkets, health food and specialty food stores.

GINGER
fresh also called green or root ginger; thick gnarled root of a tropical plant.
ground also called powdered ginger; used as a flavouring in baking but cannot be substituted for fresh ginger.
pickled pink or red in colour, paper-thin shavings of ginger pickled in a mixture of vinegar, sugar and natural colouring. Available from Asian food shops.

HARISSA a Moroccan sauce or paste that's made from dried chillies, cumin, garlic, oil and caraway seeds. The paste, available in a tube, is extremely hot and should not be used in large amounts; bottled harissa sauce is more mild. Available from Middle-Eastern food shops and some supermarkets.

HONEY the variety sold in a squeezable container is not suitable for the recipes in this book.

KALE a type of leafy cabbage, rich in nutrients and vitamins. Leaf colours can range from green to violet.

LEMON GRASS a tall, clumping, lemon-smelling and tasting, sharp-edged aromatic tropical grass; the white lower part of the stem is used, finely chopped, in many South-East Asian dishes.

LENTILS (RED, BROWN, YELLOW) dried pulses often identified by and named after their colour. Eaten by cultures all over the world, most famously perhaps in the dhals of India. **French-style** a local cousin to the famous (and very expensive) French lentils du puy; green-blue, tiny lentils with a nutty, earthy flavour and a hardy nature that allows them to be rapidly cooked without disintegrating.

MAYONNAISE, WHOLE-EGG commercial mayonnaise of high quality made with whole eggs and labelled as such; some prepared mayonnaises substitute emulsifiers such as food starch, cellulose gel or other thickeners to mimic the same thick and creamy consistency but never achieve the same rich flavour. Must be refrigerated once opened.

MIRIN a Japanese champagne-coloured cooking wine, made of glutinous rice and alcohol. It is used just for cooking and should not be confused with sake.

MISO fermented soybean paste. There are many types of miso, each with its own aroma, flavour, colour and texture; it can be kept, airtight, for up to a year in the fridge. Buy in tubs or plastic packs.

MIXED SALAD LEAVES also called mesclun; a salad mix of young lettuce and other green leaves, including baby spinach leaves, mizuna and curly endive.

MUSHROOMS

button small, cultivated white mushrooms with a mild flavour.

shiitake when fresh are also known as chinese black, forest or golden oak mushrooms. Large, meaty and, although cultivated, have the earthiness and taste of wild mushrooms.

NORI
a type of dried seaweed used as a flavouring, garnish or for sushi. Sold in thin sheets, plain or toasted (yaki-nori).

NOODLES, RICE VERMICELLI
similar to bean threads, only longer and made with rice flour instead of mung bean starch. Before using, soak the dried noodles in hot water until softened, boil them briefly then rinse with hot water.

OIL
coconut see Coconut

cooking spray we use a cholesterol-free cooking spray made from canola oil.

olive made from ripened olives. Extra virgin and virgin are the first and second press, respectively, of the olives and are therefore considered the best; 'light' refers to taste not fat levels.

peanut pressed from ground peanuts; most commonly used oil in Asian cooking because of its high smoke point.

sesame roasted, crushed, white sesame seeds; a flavouring rather than a cooking medium.

vegetable oils sourced from plant rather than animal fats.

ONIONS
green (scallions) also called, incorrectly, shallot; an immature onion picked before the bulb has formed, has a long, bright-green edible stalk.

red also known as spanish, red spanish or bermuda onion; a sweet-flavoured, large, purple-red onion.

ORANGE FLOWER WATER
concentrated flavouring made from orange blossoms.

PINE NUTS
also called pignoli; not a nut but a small, cream-coloured kernel from pine cones. They are best roasted before use to bring out the flavour.

POLENTA
also known as cornmeal; a ground, flour-like cereal made of dried corn (maize) sold in several different textures. Also the name of the dish made from it.

PRESERVED LEMON RIND
a North African specialty; lemons are quartered and preserved in salt and lemon juice or water. To use, remove and discard pulp. Squeeze juice from rind, then rinse well and slice thinly.

QUINOA
pronounced keen-wa; is the seed of a leafy plant similar to spinach. It has a delicate, slightly nutty taste and chewy texture.

SAFFRON
stigma of a member of the crocus family, available ground or in strands; imparts a yellow-orange colour to food once infused. The quality can vary greatly; the best is the most expensive spice in the world.

SUGAR
caster (superfine) finely granulated table sugar.

brown a soft, finely granulated sugar retaining molasses for its characteristic colour and flavour.

palm also called nam tan pip, jaggery, jawa or gula melaka; made from the sap of the sugar palm tree. Light brown to black in colour and usually sold in rock-hard cakes; use light brown sugar if unavailable.

SUMAC
a purple-red, astringent spice ground from berries growing on shrubs that flourish wild around the Mediterranean; adds a tart, lemony flavour to dips and dressings and goes well with barbecued meat.

TAHINI
a rich, sesame-seed paste, used in most Middle-Eastern cuisines, especially Lebanese, in dips and sauces.

TOFU
also known as bean curd, an off-white, custard-like product made from the 'milk' of crushed soya beans; comes fresh as soft or firm. Leftover fresh tofu can be refrigerated in water (which is changed daily) for up to 4 days.

silken tofu refers to the method by which it is made – where it is strained through silk.

WHITE SWEET POTATO
less sweet than orange sweet potato; has an earthy flavour and a purple flesh beneath its white skin; best baked.

WOMBOK (NAPA CABBAGE)
also called chinese cabbage or peking cabbage; elongated in shape with pale green, crinkly leaves. The most common cabbage in South-East Asia.

YOGHURT, GREEK-STYLE
often made from sheep milk that is strained in a cloth (traditionally muslin) to remove the whey and to give it a thick, smooth, creamy consistency, almost like whipped cream.

ZUCCHINI
also known as courgette; small green, yellow or white vegetable belonging to the squash family. When harvested young, its edible flowers can be stuffed then deep-fried or oven-baked.

INDEX

Published in 2017 by Octopus Publishing Group based on material licensed to it by Bauer Media Books, Australia.

Bauer Media Books is a division of Bauer Media Pty Limited, 54 Park St, Sydney; GPO Box 4088, Sydney, NSW 2001, Australia phone (+61) 2 9282 8618; fax (+61) 2 9126 3702

www.awwcookbooks.com.au

MEDIA GROUP

BBAUER MEDIA BOOKS

PUBLISHER Jo Runciman

EDITORIAL & FOOD DIRECTOR Pamela Clark

DIRECTOR OF SALES, MARKETING & RIGHTS Brian Cearnes

CREATIVE DIRECTOR Hannah Blackmore

SENIOR DESIGNER Gayna Murphy

SENIOR EDITOR Stephanie Kistner

JUNIOR EDITOR Amanda Lees

FOOD EDITOR Alexandra Elliott

OPERATIONS MANAGER David Scotto

PUBLISHED BY Bauer Media Books, a division of Bauer Media Pty Limited, 54 Park St, Sydney; GPO Box 4088, Sydney, NSW 2001, Australia. Ph +61 2 9282 8618; Fax +61 2 9126 3702 www.awwcookbooks.com.au

PHOTOGRAPHERS Ben Dearnley, William Meppem

STYLIST Vivien Walsh

PHOTOCHEFS Charlotte Binns-McDonald, Dominic Smith

COVER PHOTOGRAPHER James Moffatt

COVER STYLIST Olivia Blackmore

COVER PHOTOCHEF Tammi Kwok

FRONT COVER Mushroom, cavolo nero & quinoa risotto, page 61

Published and distributed in the United Kingdom by Octopus Publishing Group Ltd

Carmelite House

50 Victoria Embankment

London, EC4Y 0DZ

United Kingdom

info@octopusbooks.co.uk;

www.octopusbooks.co.uk

PRINTED BY Leo Paper Products Ltd, China.

INTERNATIONAL FOREIGN LANGUAGE RIGHTS

Brian Cearnes, Bauer Media Books

bcearnes@bauer-media.com.au

A catalogue record for this book is available from the National Library of Australia

ISBN: 9781742458861 (paperback)

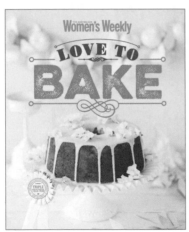
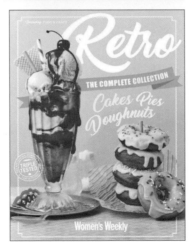